TRUMAN IN RETIREMENT

TRUMAN IN RETIREMENT
A Former President Views the
Nation & the World

G.W. SAND

Justice Books
an imprint of Diamond Communications, Inc.
South Bend, Indiana
1993

TRUMAN IN RETIREMENT
Copyright © 1993 by G.W. Sand

Manufactured in the United States of America

Diamond Communications, Inc.
Post Office Box 88
South Bend, Indiana 46624-0088
(219) 299-9278
FAX (219) 299-9296

Library of Congress Cataloging-in-Publication Data

Sand, G. W. (Gregory W.)
    Truman in retirement : a former president views the nation & the
world / G.W. Sand.
        p.   cm.
    Includes bibliographical references and index.
    ISBN 0-912083-63-8 : $19.95
    1. Truman, Harry S., 1884-1972. 2. Presidents—United States-
    -Biography. 3. United Stated—Foreign relations—1945-1989.
I. Title.
E814.S25   1993
973.918'092—dc20
[B]   93-7994
                                                           CIP
                                                            AC

CONTENTS

In Memory of My Parents

ACKNOWLEDGMENTS

This account of Truman's post-White House years owes much to the support of the Truman Library Institute and the help of a number of individuals.

I am especially indebted to Erwin J. Mueller, archivist—now retired—of the Harry S. Truman Library, whose unfailing assistance made possible my research of this neglected theme. Similarly, I am indebted to the library's director, Benedict K. Zobrist, and the Committee on Research and Education of the Truman Library Institute for the timely research grants awarded this project in 1989 and 1990.

Others, too, have helped in various ways: Pauline Testerman of the Truman Library, Maura Porter of the John F. Kennedy Library, Lorna Mitchell of the Westminister College Library, Cindy Stewart of the Western Historical Manuscript Collection in Columbia, Ted Gittinger and Regina Greenwell of the Lyndon Baines Johnson Library, Bill Olbrich of Washington University, and former U.S. Senator Eugene J. McCarthy, who, thanks to his own useful bibliography, directed my attention to some important aspects of Truman's view of the presidency. My thanks also to Francis H. Heller, Professor Emeritus of the University of Kansas, and Lewis A. Tambs of Arizona State University for their thoroughness in commenting on the initial draft of this manuscript.

Lastly, to Sue Gold and the staff of the Eden-Webster Libraries in providing anew for my research needs, I am twice indebted, as I am, again, to my wife Jane.

INTRODUCTION

Harry S. Truman, who became president during a time of world crisis, inaugurated United States participation in the United Nations, the Marshall Plan, NATO, and the Korean War, and consolidated the New Deal of his precedessor. The experience of those years would remain with him during the 1950s, a decade that journalist Theodore White views as the years from 1953 to 1963. These same years would mark the building of a presidential library to house the papers of Truman's wartime and postwar presidency, the writing of his memoirs, his continued participation in Democratic politics, and as spokesman for a bipartisan foreign policy, and active support of the cause of world peace.

Indeed, the issue of world peace increasingly occupied Truman's attention after 1963, following the tragic death of JFK, a president Truman himself had done much to get elected. Hence, in 1965, when Truman was approached by a number of benefactors who wanted to dedicate a Peace Center in Jerusalem in his honor, he welcomed the plan and soon after a Peace Center was erected on Mount Scopus, the highest hill overlooking Jerusalem, in 1970.

If the former president "did not have a grand vision of the postwar world" when he entered the White House, he did come to have a vision of the future, though he believed that much depended on the next generation to nurture and develop it.[1] His vision of a "better world," and of U.S. responsibility in maintaining it, required an understanding of the past, be believed, especially after 1920, when President Warren Harding refused to support America's adherence to the League of Nations. Truman thus held that the new generation must assume the responsibilities "of a great free nation," and "accept the world leadership...God intended America to accept in 1920, maintain freedom of thought, freedom of action, and keep this government of, by, and for the people who support it."[2]

In the same article, "The Future for Young American," published on 13 December 1953, Truman stressed that youth must be interested in their government, and that they must know "the foundation stones upon which this nation is built." He saw also the need of a general or liberal education "for every young person," arguing that a knowledge of science and technology alone would not meet the requirements of a "shrinking" world, because he felt men and women of the next generation must be open "to the opportunities that lie ahead."[3] Earlier, in this vein, in one of his last speeches as vice president, he had stated that, "Enlightened worldwide education may be the lost key to lasting peace," a statement that envisioned his most important peace initiative as president, the Point Four program to provide technical assistance, including learning skills, to developing nations.[4]

Toward the end of the 1950s, however, unhappy with the domestic and foreign policies of the Eisenhower administration, the former president was less sanguine about America's future world role. Uncertain how long it would take to achieve a better world, he was still hopeful that the U.S. would take the lead, though "it may not be," he wrote, because the U.S. had "lost some of the respect the other people of the world once had for us." "While we have lost some of that standing now," he added, "I hope we can get it back."[5]

Truman, also, looked upon the U.N. as the first step in seeking to bring about a more peaceful world since its formation in 1945. And while the Korean War early challenged the principle of collective security, he maintained that the U.N.'s future had been strengthened by the decision to save South Korea. As Winston Churchill, who applauded Truman's decision to intervene, described it: "Now the free world was not a naked world, but a rearming world."[6] And in testimony before the Senate Foreign Relations Committee in April 1955, in hearings on amending the U.N. Charter, the former president held that without the U.N. world peace would have been lost, and that "those…who helped to set up the United Nations knew that it would have a long and difficult task."[7] Truman, moreover, minced no words in citing the Soviet Union as the chief villain in thwarting efforts to achieve world peace, as noted hereinafter. Yet, he could not forget during these years to remind audiences on college campuses that the United States must assume its rightful role in the future, and warned that achieving a better world would not be attained without great effort, without wide education, nor without an understanding of the nation's history and constitutional origins. As in his Radner lectures at Columbia University in 1959, he admonished his listeners to, "Read the history of some of the great republics of the past," and, "find out what happened to them when people became fat and easygoing and failed to look after the interests...of government." He vouchsafed that if the citizenry should fail in this regard, to look out for the welfare of this great government and the Constitution, that it could be destroyed.[8]

Alas, the decline of which he spoke has seemingly followed his passing in 1972, as the two decades since then have been increasingly marked by a "widening gulf between the president and the American people," especially in the area of government's traditional public role in defending the powerless and victims of established private power.[9] Kindred gaps have also reemerged in foreign affairs—a related theme—despite the end of the so-called era of the "Imperial Presidency." Lastly, such failures appear in marked contrast to the constitutionally-based policies of former President Truman—the traditional lines of authority and accountability that he followed—and that he exercised in the face of some of the most trying decisions an American president has had to make.

Hence, the aim of this book is to understand, rather than critique, Truman's multifarious activities after 1953: his concern for the well-being of the nation and the nation's educational establishment, his concern for peace, and his efforts to present the facts relating to his wartime and postwar presidency. As he confided in a letter to Senator Richard L. Neuberger on 13 February 1956, a few months after the first volume of his memoirs appeared: "I did everything I could for the welfare of the country and for the peace of the world, he wrote...my actions and statements have been so thoroughly misrepresented, I had to tell the facts myself as best I could."[10]

Mr. Truman thus never ceased to draw upon his unprecedented experience and knowledge of those years, 1945 to 1953, in retirement, which is evident in his memoirs, his voluminous correspondence, his many speaches and lectures, his role as the Democratic Party's elder spokesman, his advocacy of reading and learning from the past, his role as spokesman for a strong defense and mutual assistance in the face of continued Soviet hostility, and, above all, his call for creating a better world through education, at home and abroad.

Not least, also, had been Mr. Truman's criticism of Republican policies between 1953 and 1960, especially when measured against the "six" duties of the president to promote the general welfare: to ensure that the laws are "faithfully executed," to oversee the nation's foreign relations, to serve as its commander in chief, to exercise such duties as required in the legislative field, to lead one's political party, and to perform a president's ceremonial duties as head of state.

It is the task of this work, then, to account for the former president's unusually strong and consistent stand on the issues involved: as to the presidency in particular, on the issues of public concern that occupied his attention and interest as a leading democratic spokesman for nearly the last two decades of his life, and as to his steadfast belief in history as a guide to conduct in providing a guidepost to the past and future of American democracy, free society, and a better world. In sum, it is such matters that seem most important about Truman's last years, and in order to understand what he was trying to accomplish and why he worked so hard after retiring from public office, we must focus on his views and deeds rather than on any frustrations and pecuniary difficulties and ill-health that ensued in the course of these years—some three weeks short of twenty years—between 1953 and December 1972.

Part I thus surveys this scene on his return to Independence, and, in large part, as it relates to his views and recollections and the building of a presidential library there; Part II moves on to the national and international scene and to his great interest in the fortunes of the Democratic Party within that wider realm; Part III intimates and ends with the better world he continued to believe in and look toward.

After their journey from Washington, 22 January 1953, President and Mrs. Truman, with the mayor of Independence and his wife. (Kansas City Star Co.)

*President
Truman
holding tear
sheets of his
Memoirs.
(Harry S.
Truman
Library)*

From left to right: Basil O'Connor, Alonzo Gentry, Harry S. Truman, Dean Acheson, and David Lloyd at the site of the Truman Library in 1954. (Harry S. Truman Library)

PART I

FROM WASHINGTON
TO INDEPENDENCE

THE FIRST MONTHS

Although Truman had once considered campaigning again for the presidency, the last weeks of his administration left few doubts as to the course he would follow after leaving the White House on 20 January 1953. In a farewell dinner given at the White House in December 1952, he remembered to invite a naval aide—his predecessor's—whom he had not seen since 1945, Vice Admiral Wilson Brown. The president, also, recalled Brown's warning then concerning increasing Soviet "misdeeds" since Yalta, a telling factor in view of the large Lend-Lease supplies in 1945 still being delivered to Stalin. While he again had the chance, the admiral thought to bring another important matter to the president's attention; namely, that he should not fail to write his memoirs while the important decisions "were still fresh in his mind." Brown recalled reading nearly all of the books written about Franklin Roosevelt, and that few of the writers had presented a clear summary of the known facts when the decisions were made; their hindsight, rather than yielding new insight, had distorted the historic decisions of those years. "I don't know what history will say about me," Truman replied. "But I can honestly say I did the best I could."[1] If anything, the admiral's remarks served as a useful reminder of the importance of such a project. If he did not tell the facts as he remembered them, the recollections of others would likely result in similar distortions about the decisions made since 1945.

In truth, the President may well have had these thoughts in mind as he addressed the nation in his farewell speech from the White House on 15 January 1953. He spoke from the Oval Office where he had worked since April 1945—where he had signed myriad documents, had made many of his decisions, and from where the presidential office followed him: to Germany, as he said, in 1945, to Canada, Brazil, and Mexico, and to Hawaii, the latter being a brief stopover in 1950, enroute to his meeting with General Douglas MacArthur at Wake Island. President

1

Truman recalled some of the many decisions he had to face with the abrupt passing of his great predecessor, as the decision to employ the atomic bomb, adding that he "made that decision in the conviction it would save hundreds of thousands of lives—Japanese and American."[2] Above all, he emphasized the Korean War decision, and that he and his advisors saw the issue as being "whether there would be fighting in a limited area... or on a much larger scale later on." The decision, he avowed, was "the most important in (his) time as President."[3]

In the half-decade then between 1945 and the Korean War, Truman's thinking on foreign policy had been much influenced by what had gone before: what had happened in the 1930s, and what had happened to American foreign policy since the defeat of Wilson's peace program in 1920. As he said on that occasion, the United States wrongly withdrew from world affairs by failing to act in concert with other peoples against outside aggression, "helped kill the League of Nations," and inaugurated "tariff barriers which strangled world trade." In brief, the decisions between 1945 and 1950 were made to arrest these post-World War I failures, beginning with the U.N., the aid program to Greece and Turkey, the Marshall Plan, the Rio Treaty, in bringing the Western Hemisphere together, and the North Atlantic Pact. The aim of "peace and safety," he hoped, would follow under U.N. sponsorship alongside peaceful developments, and that the latter would accelerate so fast that "we will not recognize the world in which we now live."

In his farewell, the president had likewise been ebullient in reviewing the state of the nation. There were 62.5 million employed, he declared, no bank failures had occurred in nearly nine years, and the nation's income had been more fairly distributed "than at any time in recent history." Neither he nor Mrs. Truman, he added, had any regrets. He had done his best in the public service, and believed that he had "contributed to the welfare of (the) nation and to the peace of the world."[4]

Truman had doubtless succeeded to an extraordinary degree. He had succeeded, in General Omar Bradley's words, because he had used his knowledge of history when he needed to. "No other peacetime President has ever been called upon to make such...difficult decisions," nor has any "other President had a better knowledge of history upon which to base his decisions," Bradley confided to the retiring president, adding that he was "confident that future historians will accord your actions the high praise they deserve."[5]

Again, those who had known the president, or had served under him during his presidency, would not have been surprised by his letter to the librarian of Congress, Luther Evans, on the eve of his farewell address in early 1953. As he wrote to Evans on 12 January: "I am expecting to maintain our close contact...because I am going to be interested in libraries and research for the rest of my life."[6]

One week later, following the inauguration of Dwight Eisenhower as president, Mr. Truman, along with his wife and daughter, had been enthusiastically welcomed by some five hundred well-wishers, before boarding their train to return to Independence, a scene that would be repeated on leaving Washington's Union Station at every stop across nearly half a continent. "It was the pay-off," Truman wrote, "for thirty years of hell, and hard work."[7] And in a speech at Independence shortly after their return, on 5 February, he reminisced on the "trials and tribulations" of public office going back to 1922, but mostly on the "rough times of service," as he put it, in the later years of "awful responsibility" as president. Still, "the hometown reception," he acknowledged, "was worth all the effort—all the trials. Never has there been anything like it in Independence in my recollection or any other ex-President's hometown." Truman reminisced, too, about his and his hometown's past: about Noland School in 1892, even recalling the cap that he wore with the names of Grover Cleveland for President and Adlai Stevenson for Vice President—the grandfather of the man he supported in 1952; about the old Independence High School he had graduated from in 1901, of which no records exist that he graduated, since it was destroyed by fire; and of Independence as the "gate-way city" in the development of the old West.[8]

Nonetheless, Truman's retirement from the presidency also marked a dramatic turnaround. He had left "empty-handed" on his return to semi-public life in Independence, since retirement benefits for ex-presidents had never been enacted into law; not, that is, until 1958. Yet he rejected any idea that might exploit for his own "personal gain" the office he had held. Thus he was unmoved by the many offers that followed in the first months of 1953: to assume the vice presidency of a clothing store at an annual salary in six figures, as chief executive of a motion picture company, and an eight-year contract at a salary of over a half-million dollars, requiring only an hour's work.[9] Such offers, one of Truman's biographer's wrote, "were manifestly attempts by second rank enterprises to buy his name rather than his wisdom."[10] So Mr. Truman also thought. To compromise the dignity and prestige of the presidential office for commercial advantage, however respectable, exceeded the bounds of propriety. Privately, however, he had been frank in expressing the need for financial help in meeting an ex-president's overhead costs; his mail alone ranged between 50 and 150 letters daily. And his only source of income at that point had been a small monthly ex-Army pension. As he would later tell House Speaker Sam Rayburn, he would need some federal assistance in order "to keep ahead of the hounds."[11]

He was thus interested in exploring a possible niche for himself in television. As long as it in no way embarrassed the presidency, he was not averse to exploring its advantages for educational purposes. To be able to share with youth his concerns about free society and talk to them about their government and history thereby won his approval. Mr. Truman had agreed to make three TV appearances, the most memorable, perhaps, being his first appearance from his office in Kansas City shortly after his return from a family vacation to Hawaii that first year. The former president had said that he agreed to participate because the purpose was educational, and that, since his return to private life, he had been besieged by "calls to talk about the state of the world, especially from young people," who worried about their future "in a time when destructive forces seem to be gathering around the globe." Despite two tragic world wars—a common reference point, as in later talks—and the changes they had wrought, Truman remained optimistic because the "world has also been strengthened by science and by the growth of this country to world leadership." He found another reason for optimism in the student exchange program since students had "obtained a greater understanding of the countries in which they had studied." These developments, he believed, along with the strengthening of the U.N.—another point of reference in his later speeches—"will be the means to create peace in the world for future generations."[12]

Apart, then, from his first TV appearance, and such matters as his memoirs and future library, Mr. Truman had been able to visit Hawaii with his wife and daughter—amidst other entreaties of one kind or another—during those first months after leaving office. As he wrote to the chairman of the Democratic Party in Hawaii, John A. Burns, in late February, he wished to absent himself from any political activity for at least six months, though he left open the possibility of meeting with "some of the stalwarts of the Democratic Party during his stay there."[13] He replied on the same day to Admiral Arthur Radford, commander of the U.S. Pacific Fleet, that their Hawaiian vacation at Coconut Island would provide "an opportunity for us to get together," a visit regarded as obligatory, along with his visit with the governor of Hawaii, Oren E. Long. [14] He had agreed also to accept an honorary degree from the University of Hawaii on 24 April, near the end of their month-long vacation. Last, though his wife and daughter were "both allergic to flying," as he told Admiral Radford, and "have no interest in volcanoes," he was "most anxious to have a look at (the) most active volcano in the world," Mauna Loa, on the island of Hawaii. [15] And though he declined other such invitations, he willingly agreed to review the First Provisional Marine Joint Air-Ground Task Force at Kaneohe Airfield on 18 April.

In his acceptance speech at the University of Hawaii on 24 April, following conferral of the Doctor of Humanities degree, he promised to say a few words on the subject of statehood for Hawaii. In that address, however, Mr. Truman stressed the importance of history as a guide to conduct. He said that he was "very much interested in the classics as a basis for education," but averred that education of the individual must be "based upon the experiences of history," without which, he admonished, the individual "has no education." The lessons were the "terrible experiences" of nearly the last half century: of the rise and fall of empires and dictators, and of the besetting circumstances of the present world, "half-free and half-slave." Yet he hoped for "a ray of light" to penetrate "the Iron Curtain so that we may have world peace; so the United Nations may accomplish the purpose for which it was founded." He seemed confident, finally, that the "rising generation" would accept the responsibility for helping to achieve a better world, and that Hawaii would "become a great State in a great Union of States."[16]

Truman's remarks on the subject of statehood that day were received with appreciation by the Hawaiian press, though his main points mirrored much of his thinking on the value of history, both academically, as the study of the past, and instrumentally. As an instrumental discipline, it had guided him as a decision-maker in the White House. And in history's other sense, his own remembrances and those of his associates, along with accompanying documents, revealed what those decisions and actions had been, and why. As he wrote an admirer from New York, confident that in the big decisions he would be vindicated, on 14 April from Coconut Island: "I think it will be discovered when history is written that we made very few mistakes in the fundamental decisions that had to be made."[17]

Homeward bound from their month-long vacation, the former president had turned sixty-nine shortly after returning from Hawaii in May 1953. He had changed his mind, however, about waiting six months before he resumed his active schedule of speechmaking as *ex officio* head of the Democratic Party. As he wrote Mrs. Robert P. Patterson, wife of his former secretary of war, a fortnight earlier: "...while sixty-nine is pretty far along, I do not feel as if it is."[18] And so, on 12 May, the former president made his first public address since leaving the White House before a Joint Session of the Missouri legislature in Jefferson City. He spoke in a reminiscent vein about the presidential office, contrasting the position of the president as head of his party and as the nation's leader in foreign affairs. He expected, he said, to have enough years left to still "be of some use to the Democratic party in the future," and in future campaigns. "I've had some of the most terrific political battles of any man alive and I'm not through yet," he proclaimed. He had refused other invitations to make speeches, he told the assembled legislators, but he could not turn down the chance to address his own state legislators.[19]

In reality then, as he had informed his state's legislators, these first months had marked the beginning of a new start as a former president. He still had much to accomplish in the years ahead.

LOOKING AHEAD

In retrospect, Truman's post-presidential plans seemed well advanced by the time he returned from Hawaii in May 1953. So, too, did they appear in being as broad as they were specific: to testify before Congress, if duty called; address issues in national and foreign affairs; engage students on the meaning of "democracy"; lecture at schools and colleges on the nation's government and history; prepare anew to travel abroad; and contribute to his party's future campaigns. His specific plans seemed no less ambitious: to build a presidential library along the lines of the Franklin D. Roosevelt Library at Hyde Park, and to write his memoirs.

As to his memoirs, for instance, after having consulted his former Special Counsel, Clark Clifford, in early 1953, as to his *Time-Life* contract to determine if his rights were adequately protected, Truman agreed to sell the rights to his memoirs for $600,000. The announcement was made public on 21 February.[20] His agreement with *Time-Life* to write a history from 1945 to 1953 was to be completed within two years, and published in late 1955. Truman, who said that he was no Winston Churchill (the last volume of Churchill's wartime memoirs was published that year), stated that he would simply be "putting his story down on paper and whether or not he could be adjudged a writer would have to be decided later."[21]

Mr. Truman avowed that he only wanted "to record the facts" that he "knew at first hand about the important events" of his administration, adding that there "was a big difference between the facts as I saw them and as they had been presented by the press and radio." So he had confided to George Elsey, his former administrative assistant in the White House: "The truth is all I want for history. If I appear in a bad light, when we have the truth, that's just too bad. We must take it." His admirable concern for the truth about the years just past, including the New Deal era, harkened back to what the so-called New England historians had written about "Jefferson and Jackson," he concluded.[22] In short, Truman was not going to have a "pack" of lies told about his years of governance and those of his predecessor.

By the end of July, David Lloyd, who had also worked for Truman in White House, sent his former "boss" an outline of the chapters for his memoirs that would focus on the presidential years. The outline, with twenty-six chapter headings, represented what they had discussed in New York along with Dave Bell and Bill Hillman, Lloyd noted, adding: "You may find it interesting— but it is, of course, very incomplete and tentative."[23] Though the outline proved helpful to Truman, and though the end product would contain no chapter headings, he was also in need of much supplementary information concerning those years. Indeed, of his need for such information his letter to Ken Hechler, a former White House aide, on 5 August, was typical. Informing Hechler that the enclosure in his letter of 27 July on "Demobilization, 1945-1946," was exactly what he needed, Truman added that "any other briefs and facts that took place around the White House" would likewise be helpful. [24]

Concurrent with his early decision to write his memoirs, Truman had wanted to see a building for the study of the presidency located in the Middle West; one, that is, that would be accessible to students from many educational institutions in that part of the country, and that would serve as an important regional center for research where none then existed. Again, plans along these lines had long been a priority, if not a preoccupation of the former president before 1953. Still, such plans had been in a preliminary stage up to that time. Thus on 5 March 1953, at a meeting of the Board of Trustees of the Harry S. Truman Library, Inc., a nonprofit organization created to raise funds for the library from private donations, Truman had "made a brief speech explaining the library project, its importance, and his hopes for its development." He talked also of "the function of the Library as a regional center for study, and its value to the history of the country." Following, in fact, Truman's remarks that day at a meeting of the library's trustees in Kansas City, the meeting focused on the fund-raising plans and the regional meetings being planned to raise the estimated 1.75 million dollars deemed necessary for its construction. [25]

10

Basil O'Connor, the chairman of the library's Executive Committee, described the various fund-raising activities and regional committees being organized to meet that goal. And at a follow-up meeting that September, he reported on the various committees for the library that had been set up around the country functioning as regional committees: in Los Angeles, San Francisco, Denver, Kansas City, St. Louis, Washington, D.C., and New York, with plans well advanced for such committees in Chicago, Boston, and Philadelphia. O'Connor also announced that the library had already received contributions in excess of $500,000; hence that detailed plans could go forward to begin construction as soon as possible.[26] An elated Truman thus wrote his longtime advisor on 2 October, Dean Acheson, in reference to the board's go-ahead: "I am having more interest displayed in the proposed Library than I ever had since it started. Two or three of the great foundations are now...interested in it."[27]

Truman had, to be sure, other public concerns on his mind that first year, most notable, perhaps, being his long held views on Republican control of the presidency, a matter of concern equalled only by his desire to help the Democratic Party in future campaigns. Of note had been his early appraisal of the Eisenhower administration, and of the new president's seeming inability to make decisions in the interest of the general welfare. Probably the earliest reference in this vein was his reply to Acheson's letter of 14 April, while he was still in Hawaii, on 24 April. "I do not see how it is possible to get things in such a mess...in ninety days," Truman wrote. "It looks as if the President is giving all of his prerogatives away..."[28] Such former cabinet members as Acheson and Averell Harriman shared Truman's appraisal. As Harriman wrote Mr. Truman on 2 June: "I hear from my Republican banker friends in different parts of the country that the President's tight money policy is drying up credit for home construction, consumer goods and farm equipment," and that even industralists are "holding up on expansion programs." Harriman added that he stressed these points in all of his speeches, with the admonition that a recession will occur unless this policy is modified. And in an earlier letter to Truman, on 15 May, he was equally harsh against John Foster Dulles' "playing of domestic politics with foreign policy"; that is, of negating bipartisanship in foreign affairs by involving "domestic political considerations with our security and foreign affairs. What you have built," Harriman despairingly concluded, "is being rapidly torn down."[29]

On 7 September, Truman's Labor Day speech in Detroit provided an opportunity he had not had before to address such issues, even though his speech was not viewed as a political one. In fact, his former aides advised him to avoid attacking "the new administration too sharply," and instead to discuss "the issues constructively."[30] Doubtless, Truman had tried to do that in a lengthy speech at the invitation of the joint organizations of the American Federation of Labor and the Congress of Industrial Organizations. He spoke, for example, of the need for unity as a free people. But he refused to yield on what he regarded as the adversarial nature of Republican rule. Though the majority of the people voted for a change in the political party, they had not voted for a change in the "social and economic principles" that have made this nation prosperous again, and strong, Truman stated. Yet there were "plenty of signs" that the government was turning its back on these principles and, correspondingly, the general welfare. The new administration, he said, had "raised interest rates across the board," a measure that benefits "the money lenders," but that hurts the veteran, the small businessman, and the "taxpayer who has to pay more interest on the public debt." And his closing remarks reverberate still as the century draws to a close: "Our strength at home is the foundation of all our efforts abroad...I don't want to see anyone take us back to the old ways of greed and arrogance, and indifference to the public weal which we rejected twenty years ago," concluding that "if those days return, we shall lose our strength at home, and our moral leadership abroad, and the path will lead to depression and destruction."[31]

As the year 1953 unfolded, Truman found no reason to revise his appraisal. Nor had Acheson or Harriman, two of his ablest former cabinet members. Though Truman could not but accept "the will of the people," he could not refrain from expressing his dissent then, or later. As he wrote in his inimitable way to Melvin Hildreth, chairman of the Democratic Party's Washington area dinner committee months later: "The plain truth is that the Republican Party leadership does not know how to conduct our government in the interest and for the general welfare of the people." Instead, it continues to be the "party of special privilege...for special privilege."[32]

CHAPTER II: AUTHOR AND LECTURER

ADDRESSES AND MEMOIRS

Next to housing his presidential papers in Missouri, Truman's determination to "set down the principal facts of those eventful years" largely shaped the first phase of his post-presidency. Still, the task of putting the principal facts on paper, he soon learned, was an arduous one. Even his great interest in Democratic politics had to taken second place, as he admitted to the chairman of the Democratic National Committee, Stephen Mitchell, in July 1953. And in a letter to Acheson the following month, he seemed even more overawed by the task. "It is a terrific job. If I had known how much work it (would be), I probably would not have undertaken it," he acknowledged. [1]

When the occasion required, however, Mr. Truman's new task did not prevent him from publicly expressing his concerns involving the larger issues in domestic and foreign affairs during those first post-White House years. And while such speeches and formal addresses tended to mirror his previous White House experiences, and so anticipate some of the themes of his memoirs, they were no less useful in helping to illuminate American political history and important democratic objectives.

Thus, in his acceptance speech that fall at the Four Freedoms Foundation award ceremony, Truman related the 'Four Freedoms' to the basic pillars of American foreign policy: reciprocal trade, a strong defense—notably the North Atlantic and Rio Pacts— and technical assistance to underdeveloped countries, the last embodying the notion of freedom from 'want.' Equally apposite had been Harriman's comments on that occasion. In honoring the former president on 28 September, Harriman had stressed the importance of freedom from want, which President Roosevelt, he said, had regarded as the most basic of all, as had Truman, in giving full meaning to the other basic freedoms: freedom of thought and spirit, and freedom from fear. As Harriman well summarized it: "Roosevelt had "understood...that with the enormous productive genius which our country had developed, we could and must accept the objective of freeing our people from want, and that only in that manner could our country as a whole prosper."[2] Truman had simply carried this idea a step further when he advocated his Point Four program of providing technical aid to other countries in need.

Other speeches and addresses followed in this vein, even though some were distinctly partisan. On 5 February 1954, for example, Truman spoke before a meeting of the Americans for Democratic Action at the request of Eleanor Roosevelt. Again, he spoke out against the politics and policies of the Eisenhower administration with particular emphasis on the perceived short-comings of its domestic and national security policies: in cutting "the Air Force program," and failing to implement changes in the laws for "tax relief" and the minimum wage. It was the type of criticism that would later distinguish his speeches in the campaigns of 1956 and 1960, in addition to addressing the differences between the two political parties. As he said in that speech, the Republican Party is exclusively the party of big business, and "always gives first place to trying to take care of the immediate, short-run interest of big business."[3] Hence Republicans incline "to the belief that leadership should be from the top and that social and economic benefits should filter downward," whereas the Democratic Party, he countered, "believes that the power of government should not be in the hands of the select few" and that "social and economic benefits...should have the widest distribution..."[4]

Of all of Truman's speeches at the time, perhaps none better reflected his interest in the past, and its lessons, than in the lectures he gave at Westminster College in Fulton, Missouri, only two months later. He had not visited the college since Churchill's justly-famed "Iron Curtain" speech there eight years before. Then, as Truman recalled, Churchill was a private citizen again and he was president; but in 1954, he was a private citizen and Churchill was again prime minister. Indeed, on 12 April, Churchill had cabled the former president, recalling his visit to Fulton in 1946, and expressed regret that he could not be present to hear his lecture on "What Hysteria Does to Us."[5] And like

Churchill's earlier address, Truman's lecture that evening, and in a second lecture on 13 April, on "Presidential Papers, Their Importance as Historical Documents," had been made possible under auspices of the John Findley Green Foundation, established in 1937 to promote understanding of economic, political, and social problems from a Christian perspective.

"What Hysteria Does to Us" doubtless showed Truman's historical perceptions at his public best. "History is filled with examples of temporary mob excitement, stirred by false or exaggerated charges, resulting in injury to innocent people," and ordinarily occurring "in an atmosphere of war…economic crisis… and irrational fear." In citing such examples from the past as the Alien and Sedition Acts, the Know-Nothing Movement prior to the Civil War, and in his implicit references to the "briefcase" demagogue from Wisconsin, Senator Joe McCarthy, Truman saw a cyclical pattern in "the return of the political bogeymen who proclaim themselves custodians of our freedom," but whose methods, if not resisted, would undermine our freedom.[6] Nor did the former president limit his comments to individuals threatened by such hysteria, since its dire effects, as he noted, extended to "some of our greatest institutions—our institutions of education and religion." In such times, he concluded, "our colleges and universities have a…special obligation to maintain freedom of thought and inquiry," the freedoms mentioned in an earlier speech on the subject. Yet the freedoms thus threatened—freedom of thought and of the human spirit—represented "our greatest strength in the world struggle in which we are involved. We cannot win our goals," he added, "by abandoning our values."[7]

And on 13 April 1954, Truman gave his second—and last— Green Foundation Lecture. Given in an off-the-cuff manner, his lecture stressed the importance of presidential papers and of the need to preserve them. "A letter or a memo considered by the President to be of no value may turn out to be the answer…to a vital question," he told his listeners. He also highlighted what had happened to the papers of earlier presidents, and what ought to be done in the future to protect them for future generations.[8]

After Fulton, however, with the exception of speeches on behalf of the library, Truman had limited his speechmaking in order to devote more time to his memoirs. Lastly, as the Green lectures had focused on the former president's interest in history, so his published address on "Presidential Powers" in May and a second published address the following year on "Foreign Policy and National Defense" came to reflect, to a large degree, the central themes of his memoirs then in progress.

The following month, in fact, in May 1954, would mark a turning point in drafting the *Memoirs*. Both of Truman's aides, William Hillman and David M. Noyes, the "team" as they were called, had tried to recruit a writer-scholar to assist the former president in its drafting. Neither had been successful in this effort, and so it became Mr. Truman's turn. Fortunately, Truman's effort to obtain the services of such a writer-scholar proved to be successful with the appointment of Francis H. Heller, an associate professor of Political Science at the University of Kansas. It had been a turning point because there were only some thirteen months remaining in which to complete the arduous task of drafting a publishable manuscript, after two false starts, of some 300,000 words.[9]

Only slightly more than 30,000 words of the memoirs had been produced by the end of April, when Heller and, for a time, a journalism professor, Herbert Lee Williams, had been recruited to resume the work of drafting the memoirs. Williams' services would end within six months, however, when an attractive teaching appointment at a major university drew him away, leaving Heller, the "team," and the former president the task of completing the manuscript. Nonetheless, some "valuable guidance" came from Hawthorne Daniel of Doubleday and from Ernest Havemann of *Time* magazine, as the latter's firm, *Time-Life*, had planned all along to publish only excerpts of the memoirs in *Life* magazine while selling the book rights to Doubleday and Company.[10]

The major problem during the next thirteen months thus centered on the fact that there was so much material to cover in the time available. Hillman and Noyes would go over Heller's draft and edit it; and, on every visit to Kansas City, "they would review with Mr. Truman the outline of the chapters that had been prepared…and revise it." When in due course the number of words far exceeded the 300,000 required in the original contract, the publisher acceded to the revised 650,000 words for the final draft of the memoirs.[11]

Still, the problem remained of what to include and what to omit. Certain topics had to be given full treatment: the election of 1948, the outbreak of the Korean War, and General Douglas MacArthur's dismissal. Truman had hoped to include separate chapters on such key subjects of his administration as U.S.-Vatican relations and on "Latin America," but because of the 650,000-word limitation, these portions of the manuscript were never included.[12]

Throughout this entire period then, despite Truman's other commitments, the memoirs remained central to his efforts. Its centrality was reinforced by his insistence "that what he wanted to do was to record the history of the time as he recalled it." For that reason also, despite the sometimes round-the-clock efforts of Heller, Mr. Truman remained the key person in the process of drafting the memoirs. Again, on that account, there were many pages and many chapters where the paragraphs were set down precisely as Mr. Truman had written them out in longhand, adding: "And that's all there is to it."[13]

The last weeks of writing and rewriting would have taxed the strength of any other man of Truman's age, but the former president, as Heller remembered it, always bounced "back from things like this"; and so he did.[14]

What, therefore, next to certain themes make the memoirs of special value was Truman's sole concern to tell the truth as he remembered it, especially as to the big questions that had been his responsibility to decide. Indeed, in looking back, three issues appear foremost: the Korean War and MacArthur's dismissal, the dropping of the atomic bombs on Japan, and U.S. policy toward the Soviet Union after 1945.

ISSUES AND THEMES

As to the first of these issues involving considerations of foreign and military policy, Truman accepted, as he noted, the only policy open to the United States and the free world if another war on a large scale was to be averted. Rejecting, on one hand, the policy of appeasement and on the other of "preventive war," he described the nation's foreign policy as a "national effort to defend ourselves and the other free nations against the threat of communist conquest."[15] That policy, best known by the name of "containment," and its corollary "collective security," had been the basis for reaffirming it with the outbreak of the Korean War in June 1950. As Jim Heath in his book on the 1960s has aptly stated it: "Under Truman the United States followed a strategy of containing the spread of Communism by using the least amount of force necessary." In essence, Truman's policy and strategy had been defensive, and would be imperilled only with General MacArthur's "general advance" on 24 October 1950 "without consultation" with the Joint Chiefs of Staff in Washington.[16]

Truman, as it turned out, had been at work on an outline of his memoirs when the Korean Armistice was signed on 27 July 1953, six months after he had left the White House. Mindful, then, of how the Korean War had threatened his administration's foreign and defense policy, he had been equally mindful of the "grave constitutional crisis" caused by General MacArthur's challenge to presidential authority and the policy of collective security, which had been the administration's policy view from the outset in answer to North Korea's aggression. As General Matthew Ridgway, his successor, has noted: MacArthur had decided that "if our allies would not stand by us in...confrontation with Communist China and the Soviet Union, we should shoulder the whole burden by ourselves."[17] Subsequently, in July 1955, when Acheson was asked for his comments on the final draft of the second volume of Truman's memoirs, *Years of Trial and Hope*, he dwelt in particular on the Korean War crisis. Replying in a fourteen-page letter to Truman, he poignantly wrote that our defeat in December 1950 had been "an incalculable defeat to U.S.

foreign policy and...the Truman Administration. If we had had Ridgway in command," Acheson added, "this would not have happened."[18] Alas, MacArthur's view of the Korean War was that of preventive war, a view that had been soundly rejected with the administration's adoption of the containment policy three years before. What should not have happened, happened. As Acheson earlier confided in a handwritten letter to the former president in March 1955: "We shall celebrate the completion of your memoirs and the anniversary...of your firing MacArthur, another of your top decisions."[19]

Among Truman's other big decisions in foreign and military affairs, perhaps no other decision rivalled either in interest or concern his fateful decision to drop the atomic bombs on Japan in World War II. It had even been something of a problem in writing about this subject in the first volume, since an historian, Morton Royce of Georgetown University, who had been helping with it found unsatisfactory the view that ethical concerns about the bomb's use had not been taken into account in 1945. And so, in May 1954, when Heller came aboard to take the historian's place, Truman confessed that Royce had refused to accept his version of the facts; that is, of having ordered the bomb's use "solely in terms of weaponry and not of ethics."[20]

In 1954 and 1955, however, the reasons behind the decision to use the atomic bomb, including the ethical issues involved, had been the subject of intense scrutiny on the part of Arthur Holly Compton, one of the key scientific advisers then to Secretary of War Henry Stimson. Accordingly, in preparing "a personalized account" of the wartime atomic program, Compton had written the former president in the hope of getting the facts about the atom bomb decision at the "higher level" of which he had "no firsthand information." He only knew firsthand, as he wrote Truman on 26 April, "the thinking that was behind the recommendations that were passed on to you."[21] Subsequently, on 21 May, the meeting between Compton and Truman dealt in detail with the strategy of forcing Japan's surrender at the earliest practical date. "About every time" he talked with Stalin, Truman told

Compton, he asked "how soon...could begin the attack by the Russian armies in Manchuria." And while it appeared that Soviet entry in the war might not be needed after all, Soviet entry on 8 August, as agreed to earlier, had been viewed as an essential element of U.S. strategy in bringing about Japan's surrender. As Compton noted: "If...the Russian attack could come together with devastating demonstrations of these new bombs, even the determined Japanese warlords might be brought to their senses." And as to the moral objections raised by some of the scientists involved over the number of casualties that would result from atomic destruction, especially in the recriminations resulting therefrom, these, in Compton's view, were "considerably exaggerated."[22] Truman thus spoke for the "majority" in maintaining that the alternative would have been far worse: "one-fourth million of our youngsters and that many" Japanese killed "and twice that many on each side...maimed for life." When, after an interval of several months, Compton again wrote, asking Truman to go over the relevant pages of his manuscript to be sure "I...interpreted correctly your memories as you told them to me," he added: "As I go over these matters I am more and more impressed by the high value to the nation of the clearest decisions you were making...as President."[23]

Yet despite publication of Truman's *Year of Decisions* in 1955, wherein he gave his reasons for dropping the atomic bombs on Japan, and publication of Compton's own recollections the following year, the flow of articles and books continued to keep alive the memory of this seemingly controversial decision.[24] Still, those who saw the alternative before them in loss of life agreed with Truman's "military" decision, as against the risk of not using the bomb to end the war. Had the opportunity to end the war by using the bomb been passed up, "it would have been necessary to continue the war," since "Japan would not have yielded easily or quickly to the economic pressure of a naval blockade," and aerial bombardment. Also important was the fact that Stalin "was poised to exploit the chaos that would have resulted from either invasion or blockade." In short, the "war might have ended with

Japanese culture destroyed and the country either communistic or divided like Korea."[25]

Truman's other big decision in foreign affairs had stemmed from the so-called Truman Doctrine speech of 1947. Originating as an address before a joint session of Congress on 12 March, it held "that it must be the policy of the United States to support free peoples who are resisting...armed minorities or...outside pressure," though the support requested was restricted to emergency aid to Greece and Turkey. In thus alerting the nation to the growing threat to the free world, the "general policy" statement in world terms had been deemed necessary in order to garner the necessary congressional support for such aid. Moreover, that the proposed aid bill was never intended to be anything more than that is affirmed in Truman's memoirs. "I believe that our help should be primarily through economic and financial aid," he wrote, "which is essential to economic stability and orderly political processes."[26] Rather than being a step toward globalism, then, the Truman Doctrine was the precursor of other emergency measures to follow—the Marshall Plan, the Atlantic Pact, and Point Four—and not the opening salvo of what came to be symbolized by the term "Cold War."[27] Indeed, as Joseph M. Jones, the State Department's chief architect of the Truman Doctrine speech, wrote to Clark Clifford at the White House, in November 1949: "The advances that have been made have been emergency actions, supported at home and accepted abroad by people afraid of communism and Soviet aggression," adding that "our friends abroad have yet to hear from our side a convincing...free world philosophy and program" that is not largely "anti-Soviet." Likewise, Hillman, along with Noyes, the other half of the "team" in drafting the memoirs, had viewed the Truman Doctrine, the Marshall Plan, and NATO, including the mobilization program involving the U.N. in Korea, all as "steps dictated by a series of emergencies."[28]

Whereas the Truman Doctrine then gave expression to the nation's defensive response to the outward thrust of Soviet power, so containment expressed the nation's new foreign policy toward the Soviet Union. Thereafter, in July 1947, following passage of the Greek-Turkish Aid Bill, and the resultant withdrawal of British forces from Greece, an account of the new policy appeared in the influential quarterly *Foreign Affairs* under the title, "The Sources of Soviet Conduct," setting out "the full meaning of the containment policy." Though Truman never explicitly discussed the new policy in his memoirs, it was not any less "real" because of that. In that authoritative article, its author (George Kennan) had said that the main element of any U.S. "policy toward the Soviet Union must be that of a...patient but firm and vigilant containment of Russian expansive tendencies"; Kennan also identified its primary task as protecting "the free institutions of the Western world" against Soviet pressure. In short, containment eschewed any idea of liberation and was decidedly pro-Western in its orientation. Unforeseen in 1947 had been the Chinese communist victory in 1949, the advent of conflict between China and the Soviet Union, and containment's later "misapplication...in Vietnam."[29] Containment's other purpose had been reminiscent of Joseph Jones proposal in advancing an up-to-date free world philosophy, and that Kennan himself viewed as essential to the national interest; namely, in order to "create among the peoples of the world generally the impression of a country which knows what it wants,...is coping successfully with the problems of its internal life...and which has a spiritual vitality capable of holding its own among the... ideological currents of the time."[30]

Lastly, next to such key issues in foreign affairs involving the burdens of leadership in times of crisis were such themes in Truman's memoirs and related addresses as the presidency, the Constitution, and the value of history in education and in public affairs, themes that Truman had viewed as paramount.

Truman, in fact, viewed the presidency as "the greatest office in the history of the world," especially as it related to serving the cause of peace and of preserving in domestic affairs the Jeffersonian tradition.[31] Preservation of that tradition—dating from 1792 and the birth of the Democratic Party that year—

remained essential, he wrote, if the nation were to "be run for the benefit of all...and not for just the special crew who has the inside track," thereby unmasking in a sentence the opposing views of the presidency. Nor will anyone "question," he added, "that that was the basic thought and practice of Jefferson, Jackson, and Lincoln."[32] The divergence was primordial to his view of the office, and nothing he wrote seemed more important than understanding these rival views of the presidency. It meant the difference, he believed, between democratic and oligarchic rule, between liberalism and reaction, between a philosophy of "good government" and bad, between real progress on one hand and false progress on the other.

"The captain with the mighty heart" had been undaunted in recalling such facts about the presidency as he had experienced and remembered them: about the president as being "the principal lobbyist in the nation" for the "welfare and benefit" of all, of knowing "where he is going and why he is going there," and of how interesting is the procedure that has to be followed...when he is trying his best to run the government in the interest of all the people." Truman thus drew a sharp distinction between the Democratic and Republican party positions on the question of party responsibility for the general welfare. Citing the divergence between the parties involving the relationship between party and presidency, the Democratic Party, he held, regarded the president as a "Constitutional leader," whereas the Republicans regarded "the President as the spokesman for a ruling oligarchy."[33] Mindful, too, that the office requires a chief executive in the democratic-Jeffersonian tradition where the general welfare is involved, and that the Republicans favor a weak president in Tocqueville's sense, the onset of Republican Party control over both Houses of Congress in 1953 seemingly validated this observation. As Truman remarked in one of his speeches at the time concerning the short-lived 83rd Congress: the Republican Congress so frustrated the President's hand that Eisenhower actually "brooded over the idea of starting a third party."[34]

Though the Jeffersonian tradition exerted a powerful influence on Truman, none exerted a greater influence than the presidency itself. Truman had never sought the office, nor had he wanted it. It had been bequeathed to him by accident in a time of world conflict. His willingness, therefore, "to shoulder the responsibility of decision-making" at a critical juncture in the nation's history marked an important contribution to the presidential office. As Sir Oliver Franks wrote—Franks had been Britain's ambassador in Washington—in commenting on Truman's *Memoirs*: "He knew far better than most presidents, what had to be done to win acceptance for a policy, what steps had to be taken to translate a decision on policy into effective action," adding that this knowledge had come largely from his own experience and his reading of history.[35] His own experience, then, and knowledge of the presidency had lent a sureness and insight to his understanding of the office and its functions under modern conditions. Yet he never wrote or talked of "giving new meaning to it," nor of allowing the role of presidential advisor to receive "a special status," as later occurred with the appointments of Walt Rostow and Henry Kissinger. While President Truman had availed himself of such academicians and scholars, they were only occasionally noticed, and never cited to support or sustain a political decision.[36] Neither had Truman identified his destiny with that of the nation or sought to "personalize" the presidential office. His only concern was the reputation of his country and not as history would remember him. As former Senator Eugene McCarthy noted: "He seemed always to know when he was President and when he was Harry Truman."[37]

Future presidents, beginning with Eisenhower, tended to confuse the two, and even to personalize the office, as Eisenhower's vice president, Richard Nixon, would do in turn: Eisenhower "by making the presidential office less than it should have been and by passing responsibility to other officials of the government"; Nixon by viewing the office of the U.S. ambassador to the United Nations as simply an extension of his office, in marked contrast to its function as envisaged by President Truman as an ambassadorship above partisanship, and of special concern to the Senate.[38]

It was, then, as a student of the presidency and of American history that Truman's writings and observations in these areas assume special value, as they had proven to be in his years of public service, and in the practice of good government. "My debt to history is one which cannot be calculated," he acknowledged, and more than anything else awakened an interest "in the principles of leadership and government."[39] In truth, he never failed to write and talk about the functions of the presidential office during the first years of his post-presidency: about the president's duties to execute the laws faithfully, his constitutional duties as commander in chief and in the conduct of foreign affairs, his duties in the legislative realm, as party leader, and as ceremonial head of state. Time and again he emphasized the importance of these six functions. He did so because he believed that they were not well understood by students, by the American people generally, or even by members of Congress. As he noted, in making plans to write a book on the presidency—one that he would never write—at the urging of William Jovanovich of Harcourt Brace: "What the Presidency needs is a continuing study and a broader understanding of its powers and duties." The need, exemplified by "the many attempts throughout our history to change and restrict the powers of the Presidency," he said, stemmed "from a basic misunderstanding of the office and the duties of the President as set out in the Constitution," the most egregious in this regard having prompted his occasional comment, as in an article he wrote for *Look* magazine in 1958.[40]

Citing the Twenty-Second Amendment to the Constitution—the amendment limiting the president's tenure to two terms in office—as the most ill-conceived since passage of the Eighteenth Amendment—imposing Prohibition—in 1919, he pointed out that the former even limited the vice president's term should he be called upon to serve an unfinished term as president, "if the one to which he succeeds runs longer than two years," adding that "in an emergency the situation could be tragic." He also cited the proposed Bricker Amendment of 1953-54 as another legislative attempt "to tie the President's hands," as it "would effectively prevent the President from making...executive agreements with foreign governments."[41]

Similarly, on the issue of constitutional amendments, and in light of "the original ideas" of the Constitution, Truman's historical-mindedness was sharply focused. He emphasized on a number of occasions that he had been " 'constitutionally' against amendments to the Constitution," and that, "When you begin amending...with every pressure group (that) wants an amendment, you won't have any fundamental law of the United States." In a similar vein, in addressing the chairman then of the Senate's Judiciary Committee, Estes Kefauver, he recalled his own state's adoption of three constitutions as a consequence of "unworkable" amendments being attached to the fundamental law, and that this "is what people are trying to do with the Constitution of the United States."[42] In short, he regarded such reformist amendments as the Twenty-Second as a "monstrosity," one of the worst ever added to the Constitution, and as bad as the "short-lived Prohibition amendment."[43]

Truman had also focused sharply on the issue of the general welfare and the nation's historic origins, as he noted relative to the Supreme Court's interpretation of the general welfare clause. As he told a group of students, it had taken 150 years for the Court to find the word "welfare" in the nation's charter, even though it appears twice in the Constitution: in the Preamble and in Article I, Section 8, where it states that "the Congress shall...provide for the...general welfare of the United States." A second point—reiterated in his Radner lectures in 1959—concerned the idea of freedom as it is enshrined in the Constitution; namely, that the ideas of freedom and of the general welfare can be held together only if the relevant documents that gave expression to them, the Constitution, the Bill of Rights, and the Declaration, remain "enshrined in our hearts and mind."[44] And while these ideas and the principles that lay behind them applied to society, they especially applied to the individual. That is, it was "good" for individuals "to be seriously interested in getting ahead in the world—really necessary that they should be determined to do so; but only in ways that are compatible with the general welfare." Ultimately, then, the problem of serving the general welfare and not merely of masking devotion to it for the promotion of special interests is one that Truman identified with the mission of the nation's schools and colleges through general education and the liberal arts curriculum.[45]

In summary, it was why he believed that a liberal education should be made available to "every citizen," why in large part he had determined to devote the remainder of his life to "teaching young people the meaning of democracy" as exemplified in the example of the Bill of Rights, why he sought to make himself available to schools and colleges in order "to lecture on American government and American history," why he sought to write a history for young people that would look at the nation's history from the perspective of each of its presidents, and why he wanted to establish an archives building in the Middle West for the study of the presidency, and as a center for research and study.[46]

To appreciate these elements of his thought is to begin to come to terms with Mr. Truman's outlook, and to understand what he was trying to accomplish during these years of fulfillment and of hope for a better tomorrow.

BEGINNINGS TO 1957

It was thus in keeping with his great interest in the presidency and in presidential papers that Truman had planned to build an institution devoted to the study of the presidency, and as an educational resource of unique importance relative to the general welfare and free society. If, in fact, this view of the presidency was then widely shared, none seemed more determined that such an institution should serve this purpose than the former president himself and his administrative assistant from 1951 to 1953, David Demarest Lloyd. Yet equally important were the approximately 17,000 voluntary contributions made by organizations and citizens alike—representing all walks of life and locales—in making the Truman Library a reality.[1]

When, as early as 1950, President Truman began to consider the subject of presidential papers, his own in particular, he had been "shocked to learn that a great amount of his predecessors' correspondence had been destroyed by their heirs or through natural causes."[2] Planning, therefore, in regard to the disposition of his papers was something that he actually lost sleep over, a rarity for a president who lost little sleep over any of the big decisions he had made while in office. As his daughter, Margaret, recalled: "The Library was in some ways an even bigger job than putting his papers in order and writing his memoirs."[3]

Library planning had had its start in July 1950, when some of the president's friends established a nonprofit corporation under Missouri law for the purpose of soliciting funds for the future library, initially planned by the president to be located on the family's farm at Grandview, Missouri, some five miles south of Kansas City, and intended only to house a small part of his personal papers. Lloyd, however, reasoned that if the president decided to write his memoirs that he would need to have the bulk of his papers nearby, a position at odds with the views of some professional historians, including some members of the president's own staff, who favored keeping the bulk of the presidential papers in Washington.⁴ As a result, Lloyd's memoranda along these lines proved decisive in persuading the president—if he needed any persuasion—to follow the precedent established by his predecessor, not only of "presenting his papers to the American people," but in seeing that they became "permanently available" to scholars and "students under convenient circumstances." Were the opposing view to prevail, "of holding down what is taken to Missouri, the future growth and usefulness of the Truman Library" would be correspondingly limited, if not endangered, Lloyd concluded. And so, in a memorandum to the president on 23 February 1952 he advanced two major reasons for establishing the Truman Library—"The first to have available in one place for your own use...the principal records of your period in office." The second, "to found a center of research and study which will stimulate scholarly activity in the institutions of learning in Missouri and surrounding states," adding that these purposes would ensure the future growth and usefulness of the library.⁵

Although the library's Board of Trustees had been largely inactive while President Truman was still in office, the board was reorganized early in 1953, with the appointment of Lloyd as executive director of the Library Corporation, and Basil O'Connor of New York, a trustee of the Roosevelt Library at Hyde Park, as chairman of the Executive Committee, and, in 1955, as board president. It was also at this time that the board announced its fund-raising goal of 1.75 million dollars as the anticipated cost of building the presidential library.⁶

While still in the White House, Lloyd as much as the president had been acutely aware that the period from 1945 to 1952 "had been one of the most critical periods of American history," and that, in consequence, the Truman Library would become the repository of an unprecedented volume of papers and documents accumulated during the preceding eight years. Hence the library's holdings could be expected to serve a "growing school" of researchers and writers of an era when the nation had begun to assume "its international responsibilities" for the first time in helping to build, it was hoped, a better world. Again, Lloyd had seemingly taken the initiative in recommending anew to the president that an advisory committee be appointed whose task would be "to guide the development of the Library" as a research center so that it would "be of maximum value to scholars and the general public."[7] The president, though heartily endorsing his aide's ideas and plans for the library, thought that he faced "a sales job" in allaying "the anxiety" of East Coast provincialists who want "to keep all of the centers of learning out of reach of the Midwest and the far West."[8]

Nonetheless, the idea of an advisory committee had found support earlier as the best vehicle for consultation on plans for the library, and Lloyd's solid recommendations for it had been acceptable, even to those who wanted the bulk of the White House papers to remain housed in the nation's capital. Thereafter, with the support of Wayne C. Grover, archivist of the United States, who thought that the advisory committee's main usefulness would be "during the formative stage" in counseling the Library Corporation on polices to be followed, Lloyd's recommendation of early 1952 led to the appointment of both regional and national personages to the Advisory Committee's panel, including such well-known historians as Henry Steele Commager of Columbia and Arthur M. Schlesinger, Jr., of Harvard, in addition to Dean Theodore C. Blegen of Minnesota, Clarence Decker of Kansas City, and Dean Elmer Ellis—later president—of the University of Missouri. Thus, by January 1953, before leaving the White House, President Truman's plans for preserving his presidential papers and other historical materials were well advanced, even though the bulk of his papers—some 1,600 file drawers of 3.5 million items— had to be transported temporarily to the Jackson Country courthouse in Kansas City.[9]

Additionally, plans for the Truman Library had been aided by an earlier precedent, the establishment of the Franklin D. Roosevelt Library at Hyde Park, and given statutory expression in the Federal Records Act of 1950. And so, on 17 January 1953, President Truman stated his intention to offer his papers to the federal government under the Federal Records Act "or as part of the contents of his presidential library if and when it should be built."[10] Slightly more than two years later, however, the whole question of centralization versus decentralization of presidential papers would be settled with the passage of the Presidential Libraries Act, which President Eisenhower signed into law on 12 August 1955. Its passage was a milestone in favor of presidential libraries, and of decentralization, in adding another major function to the National Archives and Records Service, "the supervision of the presidential library system."[11]

In retrospect, the Advisory Committee had played a key role in hastening passage of the Presidential Libraries Act. Thus, in his testimony on the subject before a Special House Subcommittee on Government Operations in June 1955, Grover, as a member of that committee, spoke in favor of "geographical decentralization" as a desirable public policy and of overcentralization as bad government policy. In virtually "every aspect of our life," he held, governmental, economic, and cultural," the values of geographical decentralization have won the minds of "most of us." Grover's argument, in fact, had been the most effective made in lobbying Congress, especially in pointing to the educational advantages such a library system should provide.[12] Grover, as well as Lloyd, had also mentioned the existence of nuclear weapons as another reason for favoring decentralization, though neither viewed the issue as being central.[13] Commager, another member of the Advisory Committee, had added a further reason—namely, "that the career and character of a historical figure can best be studied and understood in the environment in which he grew to maturity," adding that "Roosevelt should be studied on the banks of the Hudson and...Truman in western Missouri."[14]

Grover, lastly, outlined three principles which he thought should guide the Advisory Committee in its deliberations (in a statement issues shortly after passage of the Presidential Libraries Act). One, he said, should be to "avoid competition with State or local historical societies in the acquisition of historical materials"; secondly, as a federal and national institution, the library "should concentrate on the development of collections relating to national and international affairs, particularly for the period of...Truman's service in the Senate and the White House." Thirdly, as an archival center, Grover thought that the new institution "should devote itself primarily to the acquisition of original source materials...rather than printed materials."[15]

The Advisory Committee had also been instrumental as a vehicle for generating ideas, especially in the case of Grover's idea and Lloyd's assistance in creating the Truman Library Institute—an Institute, as Lloyd confided to the former president—that "would be your outlet for the effort you want to make in helping to spread the knowledge of American history and to stimulate interest in our national affairs."[16] In short, the Truman Library Institute, or something akin to it, and the research students and scholars who would benefit from its programs, had been envisioned as "the ultimate purpose of the Library."[17] In thus advancing the idea of establishing another nonprofit corporation, separate from the library's funding arm, Lloyd's proposal of February 1955 gave expression to Mr. Truman's hopes for it as an active research center for the study of the presidency, and its history, as well as in foreign affairs. That this conformed to the president's hopes and aspirations for the library cannot be doubted, as such an outlook was rooted in his views on education. As in an earlier speech at Rollins College in Florida, when he was still president, he spoke of education in future tense as "our first line of defense," and as "the most important task before us." Truman strongly held that if the nation "is to retain its freedom in a world of conflicting political ideologies, we must take steps to assure that every American...shall receive the highest level of training..."[18]

In part, then, Lloyd's draft proposal of 8 February 1955 was rooted in educational ideas meant to encourage Mr. Truman to facilitate the creation of a Library Institute. The primary objective of the Library Institute was to encourage study and research in the library's historical collections, to provide economic assistance to students and researchers in using such materials, and to act in concert with the universities and colleges in the region to advance such purposes. In sum, the proposed institute would provide grants-in-aid for research purposes, which would in turn augment, as Grover had planned, the library's own research holdings, including oral histories and collective efforts such as scholarly conferences that dealt specifically with the library's holdings and educational significance.[19]

In April 1955, at a meeting of the Building Committee of the Board, Mr. Truman had generally assented to Lloyd's ideas for the Library Institute, though the Advisory Committee, meeting on 7 May in Kansas City, thought that incorporation of the institute should await congressional legislation providing for federal acceptance of the library and the Truman papers. Such legislation, as noted, became a reality only a few months later with the passage of the Presidential Libraries Act. With such hurdles behind, leaving only Lloyd's subsequent drafting of the institute's articles of incorporation to be finalized,[20] two hurdles still remained: the choice of a site for the library, and raising the additional funds from private sources to build it.

Aside, then, from organizational and procedural issues, important as these were, what had been at issue between early 1953 and July 1954, thus slowing progress on the architectural design of the building, had been the future site of the proposed library building. No hurdles of the kind, however, had slackened the pace or efforts of the library's executive director, David Lloyd. One wonders, in fact, what Mr. Truman would have done without this man, who, with the exception of Grover, helped to achieve the president's ambitions in making possible the kind of presidential library that he had had in mind.

The Grandview site had come into question because of the lack of public transport available and because of offers made, notably at Kansas City and Columbia, that did not have this limitation. Besides, some members of the Advisory Committee had been partial to the idea of a university location for the library, as Commager had been. Thus, in a letter to Edward F. Neild, of Neild-Somdal-Associates, one of the two architectural firms employed in its design, Lloyd wrote on 10 February 1954 "that a strong possibility exists…that it will be decided to place the Truman Library either on the campus of the University of Kansas City or…the University of Missouri," adding that if the decision is made in favor of a university site, the library's design, "unforeseen at present," may be affected.[21] But in the intervening months, and not long before a decision was made on the site by the library's board, the president's hometown had tendered an offer it hoped would not be refused: "An area composed of a portion of Slover Park," roughly on thirteen and one-half acres of ground, and "set on a high promotory" not far from the president's home on North Delaware.[22] In the end, the board's decision in favor of the Independence site was made with due regard to all of the factors involved, though the president's unexpected gall bladder operation may have hastened the board's decision—however slightly—in favoring the Independence offer.

In retrospect, the first half of 1954 had been an important one for the Truman Library. Thanks to the efforts of Lloyd in Washington and of Truman himself, there was a growing awareness of the importance of presidential papers. Firstly, one could point to Lloyd's article—the first of several— on "Presidential Papers and How They Grew," published in the influential journal the *Reporter* that February, and the frequent talks given by Mr. Truman on the subject in raising funds for the library to help support the claim that because of these two men, our nation's government is once more open and accessible to the people.[23] Secondly, after months of planning, though actively beginning only in 1953-54, it was the board's approval of the library site that July which helped to focus attention on presidential papers as an important resource, especially in a time of world crisis, and of locating this resource, in Lloyd's words in "the central part of the country… noted for its tendency toward isolationalism."[24]

Thereafter, following the president's recovery, the library's activities under Lloyd's direction continued apace. Development plans for the future Library Institute, the president's own interest in preserving presidential papers, and efforts to make its output more accessible all acted as essential factors behind Lloyd and Truman's vision. Essentially, as Lloyd noted, because of the enormous gap in knowledge of presidential activities, as presidential speeches and press conferences, correspondence of a public nature with other government or foreign officials, and executive orders and messages to Congress which went unpublished except for what the press covered, as compared to the other branches of government, whose proceedings and official acts are published, it was his intent to bring the people closer to their government through the use of the documents, scholarly writings, and research opportunities the Library Institute made available.[25]

Although the ensuing period had a kind of internal logic of its own, beginning with the ground-breaking ceremonies on Truman's seventy-first birthday on 8 May 1955 and ending with the formal dedication of the library on 6 July 1957, it was the library as a national resource that continued to occupy the thoughts of Lloyd and the president. And in January 1955, when Lloyd again took up the question of the library's future with Grover, the latter expressed much interest in the president's ideas, especially his plans "for acquiring additional manuscripts and historical materials." Similarly, in writing to Truman on 5 January, Lloyd expressed the hope that the library would "specialize in manuscripts and publications related to international affairs," and reminded him of the Rockefeller Foundation's interest in financing "the acquisition of all printed U.N. papers for the Library." In closing, Lloyd added that "these are topics which we ought to talk over thoroughly before the ground-breaking so that you can announce a policy for the Library and its activities."[26] Hence what ensued were the talks with Grover and with other members of the Advisory Committee, as previously noted, that led straightaway to the creation of the Library Institute as the embodiment of the president's plans for the library as a national resource and cultural institution, as a research center for the study of the presidency, (and as this branch of government struggled through the postwar era from 1945 to 1953). As Truman had said in another address, on the occasion of his seventieth birthday, the year before: "The papers of the Presidents are among the most valuable sources…for history. They ought to be preserved and they ought to be used."[27]

In the ground-breaking ceremonies that followed, the public was given a preliminary view of the president's plans for the library. It was to be "a multi-purpose" institution consisting of an archives building; a repository for books on the Truman administration, on the presidential office, and on foreign affairs; a museum, including works of art donated by foreign governments, and historical souvenirs; and a small auditorium for the showing of films of historical value.[28]

Several weeks later, when Mr. Truman appeared on "Person-to-Person," a TV program started in 1953 by Edward R. Murrow, the occasion also gave him an opportunity to talk about the library's future. Responding to the questions of his daughter, instead of Murrow, on 27 May the president told his viewers that the ground had been graded, and that he thought the library would be completed "in about a year and two months,"adding that the total collected amounted to 1.2 million, and that "the rest is in sight." When asked how he hoped to be remembered, he replied: "I hope to be remembered as the people's President."[29] In general, this thought, too, corresponded to his hopes that the library would not only become a center of important historical research, like the Roosevelt Library, but also an institution that "will stimulate our young people to study their government and to take an active part in civic and political affairs."[30]

As the construction phase proceeded, the task of having to raise another half-million dollars had become more routinized. Lloyd, who had already developed much of the publicity for the Library, and had written a few articles about it, had discovered the most successful idea of all in soliciting funds "on a voluntary basis"—the bipartisan, community-wide, fund-raising dinner at which the president appeared personally in order to "tell what he was trying to do." As his daughter wrote of these numerous dinner engagements: "The pace he set absolutely terrified me. It would have killed a man half his age." In truth, these dinners, which were held in about twenty-five different cities, enabled the library's board to exceed its goal of 1.75 million by about two hundred and fifty-thousand dollars.[31]

Lastly, between May and November 1955, a new design had been rendered for the library. The new drawing by the architects Gentry and Voskamp, of Kansas City, had been made on the basis of plans worked out by Neild-Somdal Associates of Shreveport. It revealed a structure of "contemporary design" with a limestone exterior to house the president's historical papers and books; a gallery for lectures and films; office and work space for archival staff, scholars, and students; and an office for the former president. It differed "from earlier designs in the treatment of the main entrance" and in "the adaptation of the building to the site on which it (would) stand."[32]

THE SECOND PHASE

Dedication of the Harry S. Truman Library in July 1957, the formal deeding of the library and presidential papers to the federal government under archival management, was preceded by incorporation of the Truman Library Institute for National and International Affairs, a nonprofit agency that symbolized the mind and spirit of its founders and, substantively, of the library's broad purpose. The Articles of Incorporation, as drafted by Lloyd, announced that the institute would assist in obtaining essential research and reference aids, provide research grants to promote scholarly publications based on the library's holdings, and seek the cooperation of other libraries, historical associations, and institutions of higher learning to advance such purposes. Moreover, it would look toward the development of the "Library as a national center for study and research," and seek "to encourage public understanding of the nature and function of... Government...and the problems with which it is concerned in national and international affairs..."[33]

Accordingly, having been granted nonprofit status under Missouri law to conduct educational activities on behalf of the Truman Library, on 17 June, Lloyd announced that the first meeting of the institute's board of directors would meet on 5 July—the eve of the library's dedication. Included in the membership of the new organization—persons who had "assisted in the planning and development of the Library building"—were members of the Advisory Committee. President Truman, who presided over the meeting, had indicated his interest in the library becoming "a center for the study of the American Presidency." Thereafter, Lloyd explained the proposed bylaws of the institute and reviewed their major provisions, the relation of the Library Corporation to the institute, and noted that when the time came to dissolve the former, that the residual funds of the corporation would revert to the institute. Lloyd also broached the subject of the Rockefeller Foundation's interest in providing financial support for the library's book acquisitions. Grover, who was also present, thought that the main emphasis in such acquisitions should be in books and microfilm on the history of the presidency and on U.S. foreign relations in the twentieth century. The meeting thus ended after only forty-five minutes, but it was an auspicious beginning for the new institute.[34]

Like Grover, the president's interest in the subject of microfilming presidential papers had been a longstanding one. Only a fortnight earlier, on 21 June, he had testified in hearings on the subject before a House subcommittee. He had said, as he had on other occasions, that in contrast to the other two branches of government, only the White House did not provide an "official record (of) the decisions and actions of the President." But he also noted that because the operations of the presidency include such "functions as the control of foreign affairs and domestic political strategy,...it would be difficult, and often unwise...to publish the *reasons* for all presidential decisions at the time they were made." Yet he felt that this "is all the more reason...for preserving the historical records of the conduct of the Presidency for study and examination after the passage of time has made such study possible..."[35] And so, in addressing the American Library Association in Kansas City, on 27 June, the president spoke along these same lines. He hoped, he said, that the ALA would support his "effort to see that the papers of the Presidents...are properly cared for," adding that this was "the main reason I've been trying to establish this educational institution... in Independence." Truman's reasons for preserving presidential papers, especially on microfilm, were as admirable as important, for he saw the many gaps in American presidential history with only twenty-three presidential collections extant out of thirty-two, the need for people to be educated about responsibility for free government, and the increasing relevance under modern conditions of the presidential office in relation to the general welfare.[36]

As a result of his efforts, one of the institute's early objectives and one of Truman's own had been achieved: a Public Law was approved by Congress on 16 August to microfilm the presidential papers in the Library of Congress, exactly one month before the Truman Library and museum would be opened to the public for the first time. As House Speaker Sam Rayburn wrote the president at the time the bill passed the House: "This was a great thing for you to...think of, and I think it will be of great service... especially to students for all the years to come."[37]

Though the museum would remain an integral part of the library from the day it opened on 16 September, it remained for the institute to achieve its other objectives before opening the research room to students and scholars nearly two years later. Indeed, the institute's board moved without delay in its decision to approach the Rockefeller Foundation for grant support in October 1957. Acquisitions envisioned in its proposal were deemed essential if the library was to become a research center in the areas of the presidency and American foreign relations after 1900. Thus, in writing to Dean Rusk of the Rockefeller Foundation, the institute's board considered that the library as a research center "could make its greatest contributions" in these "closely related fields" and that if the institution "is to perform effectively as a research center in these fields, one of the first steps is to provide it with a reasonably complete collection of books and reference materials on these subjects." Hence the proposed grant request of $48,627 to include the Samuel Flagg Bemis collection, "would," the proposal added, "help to establish the Truman Library as a center of international studies," as the signers of the grant proposal believed.[38] Fortunately, for Lloyd and his associates on the institute's board, the process involved in obtaining the stipulated grant was not a lengthy one, and, in February 1958, the Rockefeller Foundation awarded the library institute the sum of $48,700.[39]

With the allocation of the Rockefeller grant to the institute, Lloyd's responsibilities in library affairs, apart from those stemming from the institute's incorporation on 29 May 1957, some nine months before, nearly brought to a close his other duties as executive director of the library's funding entity. One other funding task remained, however. Lloyd wanted to obtain a mural painting that the former president hoped would occupy the space on "the wall of the main lobby" depicting the growth of the West and its spirit, especially its democratic spirit.[40]

In carrying out this task with his usual thoroughness and

dispatch, Lloyd obtained the support of the National Academy of Design, which administered the Abbey Memorial Trust for mural painting, to help finance the painting by the noted Kansas City artist, Thomas Hart Benton. And, in June 1958, in cooperation with the National Academy, the theme of the mural was agreed upon: "Independence and the Opening of the West," which would depict the "historical events...from 1815 to 1850 when Independence served as the starting point of the Oregon and Santa Fe Trails."[41]

In retrospect, it may be that the Thomas Hart Benton mural, completed in 1961, will come to serve as a reminder of how important Independence itself had been to the growth of the democratic spirit, and, not least, because of its association with the name of President Truman. Lloyd, too, who died the following year, ought to be remembered for his part in helping to establish the Truman Library and Institute as a center for research and study of the presidency in the twentieth century, and of U.S. foreign relations since 1900.

Paul Butler, chairman of the Democratic National Committee, with Harry S. Truman, Averell Harriman, Adlai Stevenson, and Estes Kefauver in Chicago, 19 November 1955. (The Chicago Sun)

President John F. Kennedy with former President Truman at the White House, 21 January 1961. (National Park Services-Abbie Rowe)

President Truman with General Alfred Gruenther in Paris, on the occasion of his visit to NATO headquarters, 10 June 1956. (Photograph by Louis De Bea; reproduced by permission of Mlle. De Bea and the Harry S. Truman Library)

PART II

THE NATION AND THE WORLD

CHAPTER IV: THE PRESIDENCY AND THE DEMOCRATIC ADVISORY COUNCIL

THE PRESIDENCY AND THE DEMOCRATIC PARTY

President Truman's devotion to democratic ideals had strengthened the Jeffersonian tradition about the democratic nature of the American presidency in practice, if not in theory. His concern, for example, about the need to preserve presidential papers cannot be fully understood apart from that tradition. As he stated on a number of occasions, as in his Radner lectures in 1959, he wanted students to know "exactly what this situation is and what you have to do to keep it." He was referring, of course, to the presidency, though, being a practical politician, he was not given to theoretical formulations about it. Yet his meaning was clear: "You didn't get it without blood, sweat, and tears, as Winston Churchill said," he told them. "We had to whip ourselves for four years before we decided that we wanted to have the *kind* of free government that we have."[1]

Whatever, then, he had said or had written about the presidential office cannot be properly evaluated without reference to that tradition and its history as a guide to action. Though he was undeniably partisan, Truman's partisanship was rooted in historical precedent in domestic as in foreign affairs, the latter as illustrated by his views on the nation's foreign policy since 1920. Subsequently, in an era of protracted world conflict, or, as it was termed the cold war nearly three decades later, the matter of his successor assumed added importance because of the opposing Republican tradition, except for Lincoln and Theodore Roosevelt, whom Truman regarded as exceptions to the rule, of relatively weak presidents in national and international affairs.

Such concerns, in due course, led to Truman's uneasy relationship with Governor Adlai Stevenson of Illinois, whom he supported, but whose belated acceptance and campaign as the Democratic Party's standard-bearer in 1952 had lost Stevenson, in Truman's view, "at least three to four million votes." As he reviewed the election in December, however, President Truman recognized that no Democratic candidate "could have won," since the opposing candidate was not Robert Taft but General Eisenhower, Truman's former military commander in Europe and Army chief of staff before that. Unfortunately, when the issue of Stevenson's candidacy arose again in 1956, because he had failed to declare himself early as a candidate, Truman encouraged Governor Harriman of New York to seek the nomination as the party's liberal candidate. In fact, four days before Stevenson won the nomination again at the Democratic Convention in Chicago, Truman announced to some 800 reporters that he thought Governor Harriman was the "best qualified" to be president. What he meant was that the Democratic Party needed "a dynamic and fighting candidate who will not compromise on the fundamental issues," adding that the party needed a candidate who could win, and "keep the party from falling into the hands of a...minority group who would be content to act as caretakers under a Republican administration."[2] That the will of the convention preferred Stevenson to Harriman had not really changed anything or compromised the party's unity, since Stevenson had already endorsed the party's liberal platform. As Truman confided to Stevenson on 19 August, after congratulating him on the nomination: "You have all the qualifications for that position if you will just let them come to the top." He added that the "principles of the Democratic Party and the welfare of the nation...were at stake," and that the "Party cannot exist as a 'me too' Party," and "must be ready to see justice done to those who can't hire expensive representatives to look after their welfare in Washington. Only the President can do that," Truman added.[3]

And in November, despite Stevenson's failed effort to regain the White House for the Democratic Party, Truman had been magnanimous in writing Stevenson on the 21st. "You have no reason to feel bruised," he explained. "You made a wonderful campaign; only demagoguery and glamour defeated you—nothing else." Indeed, the former President was still willing, as he told a Stevenson supporter in 1958,[4] to support his nomination again in 1960, if it would be necessary to reclaim the presidency from Republican Party rule after eight years of diminutive, uninspiring, and faithless governance, as measured, in Truman's view, against the Jeffersonian tradition.

Mr. Truman never doubted that the Democratic Party must "keep up the fight." Nor, from his perspective, were his fears about Republican rule unjustified, since Eisenhower, as Truman noted, had violated an important tenet of democratic governance by allowing the presidential office to become enfeebled, against which even the *Federalist Papers* had warned. So, too, he believed, had the new administration left itself open to the charge of amateurism by attempting to "discredit" his own administration and that of his predecessor. In short, Eisenhower's presidency had strengthened Truman's observation about Republicans regarding their preference for weak presidents; that is, in rejecting "the idea of the President as the political leader of the nation" in favor of the presidency, as Grant expressed it, as a "purely administrative office."5

In principle, though Truman loathed the idea of criticizing the new administration's foreign policy, he was not at all reluctant to do so in domestic affairs, especially on issues relating to the general welfare. Privately, however, he drew no distinctions between the two, as his letters bristled with dissent against an administration he saw as wrecking prudential policies at home and as maneuvering to overturn established foreign policies since the New Deal era. Specifically, he decried Eisenhower's "tight money" and agricultural policies and the administration's apparent abandonment of bipartisanship in foreign affairs and the Good Neighbor policy.

But there was more. Truman was appalled, for example, by Eisenhower's seemingly "do-nothing" approach to the presidency in the face of the fact that "the President cannot evade responsibility nor delegate his duties to others." He further noted in his foreword to the text, *Politics, 1956*: "The failure to face up to decisions can be as dangerous as hasty and ill-advised action." Consequently, Truman believed in the president's need for advice from "many highly qualified officials, both civil and military," and stated that "if he is prudent, he will deliberate with Congressional leaders of both parties, not only on the inception of policy but on its execution."[6] Truman, finally, crossed the line on criticizing openly the president's policies, where such policies involved the president's responsibility in decision-making, especially in foreign affairs. Reminiscent of his whistle-stop campaign of 1948 was an address in Des Moines in April 1956, when he compared Eisenhower's leadership to the "do-nothing" Eightieth Congress of 1946 and 1947. Though his address focused on the "betrayal" of the farmer, he did not stop there, adjudging Eisenhower's foreign policy in the same light. In its deliberations, he added, the administration had "made a mockery of bipartisanship in foreign affairs" by putting politics first and the national interest second, and that the "result has been to dismay our friends, comfort our enemies, weaken the position of the free world, and drive other nations closer to the Communist bloc."[7] As Acheson had confided to the former president toward the end of Eisenhower's presidency: "I wonder where the world would be—or rather, I don't wonder, I know—where the world would be now if you had had the spirit of Camp David from 1945 to 1953?"[8]

Understandable, then, had been Truman's near obsession with the fortunes of the Democratic Party when it adhered to its Jeffersonian origins by guiding the presidency in promoting the general welfare and, in both foreign and domestic affairs, the national interest. Only strong presidents had seemed capable of making decisions in the interest of both the general welfare and national interest, and those, almost invariably, he believed, had been made by Democratic presidents.[9] Thus was revived the idea of an Advisory Committee or Council to facilitate that outcome in planning for the 1960 presidential election.

TRUMAN, STEVENSON, AND THE ADVISORY COUNCIL

The idea of a "shadow Cabinet" had been aborning for a number of years, at least since the defeat of Stevenson's campaign in 1952. Its intellectual rationale had also been aborning since publication of a lengthy report of the Committee on Political Parties of the American Political Science Association, published in 1950, titled, *Toward a More Responsible Two-Party System*.[10] In particular, the "Finletter Group"— named after former Air Force Secretary Thomas K. Finletter's unofficial policy planning group between 1953 and 1956—had been a useful mechanism in preparing material for the 1956 campaign and expectant post-Democratic Party victory. Still, there were other factors that came to influence the establishment of such an advisory body at the national level in view of the Democratic Party's long history as a loose confederation of state, county, and local organizations.

Foremost, in fact, was "the power struggle" that ensued between congressional Democrats on one hand and presidential Democrats on the other as a result of the party's congressional victory in November 1954, since that victory placed control of Congress in the hands of southern Democrats with Sam Rayburn as House Speaker and Lyndon Johnson as Senate Majority Leader. A second factor, inspired by Stevenson's forthright campaign, resulted from the arrival of a new class of people into Democratic organizations made up of young lawyers, writers, and professors. A third factor, and one that had troubled Stevenson during the campaign, owed to the Republican Party's "effective job of minimizing and misrepresenting the Democratic record." It had been a factor, as Truman's former Solicitor General, Philip Perlman, noted, that enabled the Republicans "to take full advantage of the opportunities offered...by an overwhelming Republican press, and...so-called news programs."[11] Not least, also, had been the fraudulent charges made by Eisenhower's vice presidential nominee, Senator Richard Nixon. Indeed, its ominous proportions would not become fully apparent until twenty-two years later, when the electorate would "discover Nixon's vast capacity for fraud."[12]

The power struggle between these two factions of the Democratic Party had not been assuaged by the appointment of Paul M. Butler of Indiana as the new chairman of the Democratic National Committee in December 1954. If anything, the new congressional leadership in the Eighty-Fourth Congress "had gone out of its way to protect the Eisenhower administration from the consequences of its own folly." Interestingly, the House Speaker had acknowledged this fact in an article written for the *Saturday Evening Post* nearly two years later, though in fairness to its author, the Speaker made a strong case against Eisenhower's so-called "dynamic conservatism," while strongly supporting Stevenson as the authentic voice of Jeffersonian democracy on the eve of the 1956 national elections.[13] And though Stevenson would again be defeated, he had waged, party leaders thought, an eloquent campaign in addressing the needs of the nation that the Eisenhower administration had either ignored or did not care to address adequately.

As a result, Stevenson became convinced that the Democratic leadership in Congress "had failed to sharpen the issues" and thus could not be relied upon to serve as the only voice for the Democratic Party in opposition. Thereupon, in late November, in conversations with Finletter and others, it was decided that an advisory group should be created to guide and make policy in planning for the national elections in 1960. Thus was launched, with the strong support of President Truman, the Democratic Advisory Council, or DAC, with the announcement being made by Butler on 27 November 1956. In general, the council thus became the instrument of the non-southern presidential wing of the Democratic Party, and, in particular, of the friends and supporters of Stevenson as titular head of the party.[14]

In addition to Stevenson, the DAC's membership boasted such names as former President Truman, Averell Harriman, Eleanor Roosevelt, Senators Hubert Humphrey, Estes Kefauver, and John F. Kennedy, though the latter did not join the council until much later. Not surprisingly, neither Rayburn nor Johnson would join the Advisory Council—Rayburn on principle, Johnson less on principle than on his Machiavellian personality.[15] As President Truman wrote Butler in late 1956: Rayburn would not "sit in on Cabinet meetings...on the basis of his legislative belief in the independence of the executive and legislative branches"; hence his "objections to being on a political committee while he is Speaker of the House"; but that in his informal meetings with Rayburn, he added, they discussed everything, and "believe you may expect the same sort of cooperation from him now, despite his decision not to serve on the Advisory Committee." By contrast, in his letter to Governor Harriman only a fortnight earlier, Truman was less sanguine about Johnson's unwillingness to support party principles. "I think our objective is to keep the Democratic Party headed in the right direction and not let it wind up with a 'me too' compromise approach as the leader of the Senate Majority would like to see it do," he wrote.[16]

By and large, the ongoing work of the council had been conducted by the council's Administrative Committee, and, except for Butler, comprised of former Truman administration officials: Finletter, was Air Force secretary, 1950-52; Philip Perlman, formerly Solicitor General; Henry Fowler, who served on the National Security Council; and Charles S. Murphy, who had succeeded Clark Clifford as Special Counsel in 1950.[17] To Murphy, in fact, together with Finletter, Perlman, Butler, and Charles Tyroler, the council's executive director, fell the task of drafting the council's Plan of Operations. Subsequently, on 15 February 1957, by a resolution adopted by the Democratic National Committee, the Advisory Council was officially established with the National Committee "pledging its fullest cooperation and support."[18] The council's operational plan, as well, had received the National Committee's "full and vigorous support in assisting (its) Democratic Members of the Senate and...House in carrying out those portions of the platform which require legislative action."[19] So while the council was generally viewed as the voice of "the presidential party" in the Democratic Party, the council also wanted to be a bridge to the "congressional party" and, at least to some extent, its southern Democratic wing in the Congress.[20]

In the main, then, in following its operational plan, the Advisory Council moved ahead with the organization of committees to prepare a series of authoritative pamphlets within the two broad areas of "National Economic Policy"and "Foreign and Military Policy for Peace and Security"; and, in a series of pamphlets under the heading of national economic policy, such themes as Human Welfare and the Public Conscience, Farm Policy, Labor, Education, Poverty, Housing and Urban Life, the Suburban Community, Natural Resources, Transportation, Equitable Taxation, Monetary Problems, and Anti-Trust Policy were focused on.[21] In addition, the council also generated such key policy reports as *The Democratic Task During the Next Two Years*, an omnibus statement adopted by the council in an all-day meeting in Washington on 7 December 1958.

The latter report had noted that in the national elections since 1954, the electorate had returned Democratic majorities in all three elections; that the outcome had been unprecedented in congressional history, and thereby "imposed an unprecedented responsibility upon the Democratic majority." The report went on to note in some detail what that responsibility entailed: a policy that would restore the confidence of the nation's allies in its foreign policy, and that would not allow "broad" and "vague and imprecise extensions" of the president's "discretionary power to use the armed forces"—a statement that envisioned what arose some six years later concerning the Tonkin Gulf resolution—and that would provide for the nation's security through advancing human well-being as its "ultimate objective" rather than through military expenditures per se. Consequently, the report noted the need for expansion of "technical assistance," annual increase of the Development Loan Fund over half a decade, and expansion of Public Law 480 to enlarge U.S. agricultural "surpluses to help needy people overseas." The report was equally firm on the issues in domestic affairs in recommending new measures to achieve economic growth in lieu of the Republican record of extremely low growth during Eisenhower's first six years (1.3 percent annually) compared to the last six years under Truman (over 4 percent annually). Also noteworthy was the report's almost strident call for a federal scholarship program during the next decade, the strengthening of civil rights legislation, an increase in the minimum wage and in public assistance to states, expansion of "long term credit and equity capital" for small businesses, development of a program to preserve family farms from the "overwhelming encroachment by corporate-type farming," and other measures to benefit the nation's economic well-being.[22]

Truman, for his part, had warmly endorsed the council's nearly unanimous approval of that report. As he wrote Michigan's governor and DAC member, G. Mennen Williams, on 30 December 1950: "Our statement from the Advisory Council was, I thought, one of the best ever made on the subject..."[23] Of Truman's own role on the council, as Murphy expressed it, it was his conviction that one of the main purposes of the council was "to keep the Democratic Party liberal," and his role as a member of the Advisory Council "was his contribution to doing that."[24] Again, that Truman was greatly concerned with keeping the Democratic Party liberal was apparent from another letter he addressed to Governor Williams in January, saying that he did not "want to see a situation develop as it did in 1924 under practically the same circumstances," adding that "William Jennings Bryan was exactly right when he made the statement that when the economic royalists get control of the Democratic Party they always take it to defeat."[25]

Truman's conception of liberalism thus becomes quite clear, when the term is viewed in its broadest sense—what some writers refer to as "ideal" or "ecumenical" liberalism—as being virtually identical with the term "democracy." That this was President Truman's understanding of liberalism cannot be doubted, and explains his interesting digressions about those he called "synthetic liberals" and "economic royalists"; those opposed, that is, to the tradition of Jeffersonian democracy.[26] It had been this broader conception of liberalism, moreover, and what it ought to mean that had been so effectively utilized in 1948, and would again be in 1960.

Hence, even before the approaching presidential convention and campaign of 1960, prevailing liberal themes were much in evidence in his letters and speeches, and expressed in contrast to what he called the "new feudalism," and those he identified as synthetic liberals. The growth of the new feudalism, he wrote, represented a threat to the nation's liberal tradition by encouraging bastions "of private power, beyond democratic control," and "exerting greater influence over our national life…and strangling individual enterprises. Liberals," he added, "can serve their country by devising means to reverse this trend."[27]

Truman, therefore, remained adamant in his determination to regain the presidency for the Democratic Party, irrespective of the good fortune of Democratic majorities being elected to the Congress between 1954 and 1958. The Advisory Council, he knew, could help but he also knew that it could not do it alone. As he confided to another DAC member, and California's governor, Edmund "Pat" Brown, at the beginning of 1959: "With a strong Democratic majority…and a good man in the White House, we can return this country to its position as the leader of the free world," adding that, "That is the principal thing in which I am interested."[28] And so it would be, as it became his consuming interest for practically the next twenty-two months, apart from his ongoing activities associated with the Truman Library and, to a lesser extent, his attention to the work of the Advisory Council until it became inactive at the Democratic National Convention in 1960.

It is of interest in this regard, besides Senators Humphrey and Estes Kefauver, who had early joined the council, that Senators Stuart Symington and John Kennedy did not become members until 1959. Interesting also was Truman's preference for Symington as the party's candidate, a fellow Missourian and former Truman administration official, as his interest in Stevenson's candidacy finally waned.[29] Still, Truman's support notwithstanding, the key to his attitude remained as it had been since 1952: he wanted a candidate who could win, and who could be depended upon to return the nation to its democratic traditions and policies in domestic and foreign affairs.

CHAPTER V: ELDER STATESMAN AND
PRESIDENTIAL ADVISOR

THE PRESIDENCY AND PUBLIC POLICY

The bipartisan foreign policy had been essential to President Truman's outlook in his search for peace, and remained so for him throughout his post-White House years. It had, for instance, accounted for his appointment of Senator Warren Austin, a Republican, as the first U.S. ambassador to the United Nations in 1946—an appointment he viewed as invaluable, as being above partisanship, and of "special concern to the Senate."[1] Bipartisanship had stemmed from America's earlier debacle and bitter partisan opposition to the League of Nations in the Senate, and had not taken root again until the Bretton Woods and Dumbarton Oaks Conferences of 1944, when U.S. delegates to these conferences were represented by both parties and held frequent consultations on a bipartisan basis at these wartime conferences. Bipartisanship, therefore, had established two key principles: first, that it was essential to national unity in time of peril, and, second, that it include the leaders in Congress of both political parties.[2] Indeed, the policy had aided the U.S. initiative in establishing the United Nations, and, as soon became apparent, in the passage of emergency measures to counter the new threat to peace and postwar reconstruction posed by Soviet adventurism and Moscow's obduracy. Truman thus became the first president—thanks to bipartisanship and U.S. participation in the United Nations—to preside over the end of American isolationalism. But did that newfound responsibility matter-of-factly confer on the presidency a "global" peacetime dimension?[3]

The advent of a Republican administration in 1953 would not diminish the former president's visibility in this politically sensitive area of public policy, despite Eisenhower's aloofness toward him and failure to seek his counsel. Acheson, for his part, spoke directly to this impasse when he wrote that during the entire "eight years of his Presidency, I was never invited into the White House or...the State Department or consulted in any way," adding that "this involved no invidious comparison since my chief, President Truman, was treated the same way."[3]

At issue, then, was not the former president's visibility but the lack of any administration initiatives in foreign policy, except, in the narrowest sense, in ending the Korean War. As to the dearth of any real policy, one of the first of Eisenhower's addresses was symptomatic, entitled "The Chance for Peace," signaling the new administration's "desire for peaceful coexistence with the Communist world."[4] As Emmet John Hughes, who authored it, wrote: the new president told him that everyone was tired of the "indictments of the Soviet regime," and that just one thing mattered—what the United States could "offer the world," adding that it came down to a choice between an arms race and disarmament. In reply to Hughes' query as to what should be said about the Soviet government, Eisenhower added: "The past speaks for itself. I am interested in the future. Both their government and ours have new people in them. The slate is clean. Now let us begin talking to each other." Hughes, who had been a key speechwriter during Eisenhower's 1952 campaign, would resign a few months later, a "disillusioned" man, though foreign policy alone was not the only reason for his disillusionment. Hughes had also been frustrated in his effort to get the president to contain the new hysteria; that is, McCarthyism. Like "The Chance for Peace" address, he wrote, the president refused to act.[5]

One of the bipartisan issues that concerned Truman had most feared, and McCarthyism was one, was the danger of disunity should the American "people...be split into fiercely partisan groups over issues of foreign policy," as he emphasized in a speech on the subject of "unity and bipartisanship" at the National Press Club in May 1954. He, too, had hoped that the new president would seize the initiative in muzzling those, as he said, who would use the "weapon of political assassination" and thereby threaten the future of bipartisanship and of American unity in foreign affairs. That the president did not take action seems paradoxical, since Eiscnhower avowed to support the "bipartisan approach" in his letter to President Truman on 7 November 1952.[6] And in that same address, Truman gave frank expression to the other cardinal point of American foreign policy, when he concluded: "Let us support...the other principle for which so much has been done and suffered in Europe and Asia—the principle of collective security declared in the United Nations Charter."[7]

In practice, then, bipartisanship served two important functions: in supporting U.N. measures whenever, in Truman's view, the free world would need to support the principle of collective security, and, as previously noted, in preserving national unity whenever it appeared that such unity over issues involving foreign policy might be threatened. In short, its purpose was to serve the national interest in time of crisis, and not weaken it either through "unilateral action" on one hand or by a return to isolationalism on the other.[8]

In April 1955, some eleven months later, Truman testified before Senator George's committee—Walter George was then chairman of the Foreign Relations Committee—involving the committee's review of the U. N. Charter. As Democratic leaders had been outspoken in their criticism of the administration's Formosa policy, and Asiatic policies generally, there was some concern among Truman's former White House aides that his testimony should not add to this chorus of criticism, should any questions about Formosa, Korea, or Indochina be raised. George, himself, had become a strong supporter of Eisenhower's Formosa policy, though his support had also contributed to his decline in popularity among his conservative Democratic constituents back home in Georgia.[9] Nonetheless, in his appearance before the George Committee on 18 April 1955, Truman did not overlook Korea in his prepared remarks. The Korean War, he affirmed, had been a direct challenge to the U.N., adding that for the first time in history, "an international organization organized effective...resistance to armed aggression." As reaffirmed in his soon-to-be published memoirs, the decision had been taken because there was no suggestion "that either the United Nations or the United States could back away from it."[10] When asked why no more than sixteen member nations had contributed forces in opposing the aggression in Korea, in view of the disproportionate number of allied forces to U.S. forces, approximately 45,000 to

450,000 U.S. service personnel, Truman replied that "the principal reason that a great many of the nations did not make military contributions...was due to the fact that they were not financially able to...and...that when the prosperity of those nations is increased... they...can contribute more to the United Nations..."[11]

As to amendments, a key issue in the hearings, Truman thought that a Bill of Rights similar to the first ten amendments of the U.S. Constitution should be attached to the U.N. Charter. And while he was sure that the Charter was susceptible of further improvements, he generally cautioned against "trying to get improvements at [the] time," adding that "we ought to be extremely careful not to loose what we already have in the United Nations, because what we have now is...essential to world peace." Yet his persistent hope for the U.N., apart from its common security aspects, related to his continuing interest in its economic and social agencies as a means of dispensing technical and economic assistance to needy countries, and, as he said on that occasion, he hoped that the U.S.-U.N. technical assistance program would not be "cut." Similarly, he regarded the Economic and Social Council as an outstanding feature of the Charter in its emphasis "upon international cooperation to promote higher living standards, full employment, and...social progress."[12] Thus Truman's emphasis on economic and technical assistance rather than on military aid recalled Point Four, his earlier "bold new program" that envisioned "making the benefits of...scientific and industrial progress available for the improvement" and benefit of developing countries. That this emphasis, also, was quite different from the new administration's preference for military aid seemingly followed from Eisenhower's dislike of Point Four, as he had told President Truman in reporting on his trip to Europe in 1952.[13]

Subsequently, in June 1955, Truman addressed the U.N.'s tenth anniversary meeting of the signing of the U.N. Charter on 24 June; and for those who recalled and warmly remembered his address in San Francisco ten years earlier, at the close of the first U.N. meeting in June 1945, his address then would again prove memorable. As in his congressional testimony that spring, he referred to the Korean decision by saying that the "decision to fight for this great organization has cost us much blood and treasure," but that it was the "right decision" at the time. So, too, had he identified the principles, he thought, that ought to guide its members in its deliberations: the principle that force and the threat of force between nations be seen in an age of nuclear weapons as intolerable instruments in the settlement of disputes, and, its co-principle, that mankind's common life carried with it a "common responsibility for the welfare of all."[14] Perhaps Churchill's letter to Truman a few days later on his retirement from public office best expressed this sense of common responsibility, when he wrote: "The decision that confronted you at the opening of the Korean War was...doomed-laden," adding that, "The great courage with which you faced it is...to a great extent responsible for the degree of easement we may now happily detect in the world. This and the building of NATO...must assure your lasting reputation and the gratitude of the free world."[15]

In September, Truman reiterated his strong support for the U.N. Organization's efforts on behalf of world order, as he told the 35th Division Association reunion at the Hotel Marion in Little Rock. The failure to "support and maintain the United Nations," he warned, "would lead to the destruction of civilization." Indeed, as he had said in San Francisco in June: "The United Nations is a beacon of hope to a world that has no choice but to live together or...die together."[16] In sum, Truman's strong support for the U.N.'s mission—not to mention bipartisanship—contrasted sharply with the Eisenhower administration's "tendency to unilateral action and concentration on military aid," as Senator Wayne Morse, a former Eisenhower supporter, reminded Truman, adding that in his Portland speech he "might want to discuss foreign policy with an emphasis upon the United Nations and economic aid."[17]

Truman, in fact, had further opportunity to discuss these matters in hearings of the Foreign Relations Committee in April 1957 on issues relating to the mutual security or foreign aid program. And though he took the occasion to highlight the history of U.S.

foreign relations, he also commented on the contemporary predicament of American foreign policy; to wit, that the Soviets were behind "all of our difficulties." As he said, in his review of U.S. foreign relations, on reaching 1945: "Let us retain our containment policy *as far as Russia is concern.* Let us listen to every peaceful program they offer, but be sure that they cannot do again what they did at Potsdam," adding that, "We do not want to give up our guns until we know that they have given up theirs." Nonetheless, the most important part of his testimony dealt with economic issues, as his statement that "in the long run economic aid is more important than military aid," and his belief that if the U.S. "can establish a peace program where everyone has everything he needs, we won't have to support a great military machine."[18]

In 1960, the former president once more addressed the U.N. on the occasion of the fifteenth anniversary of its founding on 26 June. Again, he underscored the obligation of its members not to use force except in defense of the Charter, and that, next to peace, their common obligation must be the improvement in living standards which the Charter upholds in "safeguarding the freedoms and…dignity of men." And though he hoped that the world body would organize an "international police force" to be at its disposal in time of need, his speech focused on the liberal and humanitarian aspects of the Charter, particularly as to technical assistance, adding that the only real question was—"how big should such a program be?"[19]

Loyal Jeffersonian that he was, Truman's dedication to social and economic progress abroad, and bipartisanship in foreign affairs, were matched by his equal concern at home on issues involving the social and economic well-being of his countrymen, and expressed through his efforts on behalf of the Democratic Party. Most memorable, perhaps, during these years, was his testimony before the Banking and Currency Committee of the House in April 1958. Stemming from the earlier recession of 1953 and 1954, he had been unstinting in his criticism of Eisenhower's agricultural and fiscal policies, and the new recession of 1957 and 1958 appeared to validate his earlier criticism of these policies. As he wrote to Lyndon Johnson on the eve of the new recession: "This tight money program of the special-interest people has almost put a stop to home construction and industrial expansion. The powers that be," he added, "abolished the Reconstruction Finance Corporation because it prevented a tight money market, and unless Congress takes some constructive action in the matter, we will continue down the road to another 1929."[20] Some months later, as the second recession of Eisenhower's presidency worsened, an agitated Truman confided to his former White House counsel: "My only objective is to save the Democratic Party as the party of the people, the people who have no pull at the seat of the mighty." If we cannot do that, he confessed, "we might just as well turn over the country to Wall Street and be done with it."[21]

The former president minced no words before the Banking and Currency Committee on 14 April 1958. He regarded the recession, he said, as "very serious," and maintained that the root of the problem was the administration's departure "from the philosophy of 'maximum employment, production, and purchasing power' set forth in the Employment Act of 1946." He proposed that a number of remedial steps be undertaken, including revision of "the tax structure so as to reduce by about $5 billion the amount of taxes imposed on middle-and low-income families," and an increase in revenues of $1.7 billion for fiscal year 1959, with the bulk of this being allocated to education, public health, and public assistance. He noted that in all his years as president there was no time that he "did not propose a more effective...anti-inflationary program than in fact was adopted." What was needed, he added, was equity. "The tight money policy and other restrictive fiscal policies...have not been...hard on the big corporations. But these policies "have made it much harder for small business concerns to get money"; hence the need, he urged, for remedial "legislation to provide additional equity for small business."[22]

"Eisenhower," Truman thought, "had the best chance in the world of any President to change things"; he could have worked for change instead of attacking the previous Democratic administrations; he could have developed "new policies" that would have been to his credit; he could have left "good policies alone" and changed those he did not like. But none of these things happened, Truman asserted, because Eisenhower could not make decisions in the general welfare independent of Congress.[23] He even doubted "that the Executive Department understands national finance, international relations, or national defense," as he confided to Senator Johnson, adding: "If Congress held a series of hearings—and it should—you would find out exactly how little they do know."[24]

When Eisenhower acted, however, as in the case of Indochina, and against the advice of Winston Churchill—the latter was again Britain's prime minister—by sending "military advisors" and "military observers" into that divided country, he acted contrary to American tradition. Similarly, Truman approvingly quoted from *A Pocket History of the United States*, by Commager and Allan Nevins: "When in 1954, the French departed," and the U.S. moved in, neither the interest nor the nature of the American "commitment was entirely clear." Indeed, Truman had doubted that Eisenhower and his people had thought the whole thing through, adding that he doubted "that they gave any thought to the far-reaching consequences."[25] Wayne Morse, in his letter to Truman in March 1955, felt much the same. "As I said in a speech in New York the other night," he wrote, "you always kept our country within the framework of international law, referring to Eisenhower's Asiatic policies, but that "this Administration, through the fumbling of Dulles and the ill-advice which Eisenhower is following, has taken us outside the framework of international law."[26]

Still, the norm was the reverse, Truman asserted, and not the other way around. "Eisenhower really didn't want to *do* anything or *decide* anything," he reasoned. So, too, had Acheson regularly thought. "Mr. Eisenhower, like a weary fighter, is maneuvering for the bell; and, whatever happens, he will do nothing about it, leaving these problems for his successor," Acheson wrote to his former chief on 23 May 1960.[27]

Alas, had not the most dramatic instance of failure on the part of Eisenhower to act concerned the question of Cuba between 1957 and 1959? Sherman Adams, who knew his habits best, said that Eisenhower was not much of a reader, preferring "to get his information from talking with people who knew the issues involved in the matter he was considering." He meant, of course, through direct talks, since Eisenhower according to Adams, disliked using the telephone.[28] Accordingly, when William D. Pawley, who knew Cuba well, met with Eisenhower he sought to persuade him that Fidel Castro should not be permitted to come to power in Cuba. Pawley, who had been U.S. ambassador to Peru and Brazil, attested that he held "four or five meetings with President Eisenhower in an effort to persuade him" along these lines.[29]

TRUMAN, KENNEDY, AND THE PRESIDENCY

With the approach of the 1960 presidential election, Truman seemingly had redoubled his efforts to discuss and write about the presidency and public affairs. The perceived failures of the Eisenhower years, though conforming to Truman's expectations of Republican Party rule, provided an added incentive to discuss public policy. Thus, in a letter to Walter Reuther, president of the United Automobile Workers Union, Truman wrote that "we must come up with new ideas for the welfare of the country and...the world," since the nation "for too long" has been without "constructive ideas."[30] And in a letter to a member of the Democratic Advisory Council in March 1958, he seemed confident that the council would be able to help in providing assistance along these lines. Again, though earlier, Truman had written in a similar vein to Perlman concerning the latter's statement on "civil rights."[31] In truth, some of Truman's letters between 1957 and 1960 rank among his best in discussing public policy, ranging from bipartisanship and the Twenty-Second Amendment on one hand to presidential leadership and issues involving labor-management relations and public finance on the other. His letter to Wayne Morse in November 1959—Morse, an ex-Republican, had changed his party affiliation in 1955 after a two-year interval as an Independent—spoke volumes on an issue of great importance to the future of American democracy, when he noted "that when people obtain too much power...it is a very good thing to place a check on this power." You can see what happens, Truman recalled, "when people obtain too much money too suddenly, such as...the railroad management in older days and what happened to the bankers in New York is happening again."[32]

A student of politics and politicians, Mr. Truman viewed with concern so-called "counterfeit politicians," as he referred to the right-wing politician. He had talked about such politicians, for example, in a Democratic meeting in Chicago when he said that the party had "no business going to the right. No right-winger ever thinks of the welfare of the people," and reaffirmed that "the Democratic Party is the people's only champion."[33] His friend and literary agent, Hillman, doubtless felt likewise. As Hillman noted in his letter to Truman in March 1958: "The trouble is that there are not enough politicians in the country... who...want to serve the people as a real politician should be constituted. What we have too much of," he wrote, "are...wealthy men who want more glory or power...bored individuals...who are tired of their own business and want a bit of nose-in-the-air participation in politics or...just plain thieves who want to line their pockets...and never will be politicians."[34]

Power, then, especially the misuse of power for public ends, likewise concerned Truman, and this issue was of special concern to him relative to economic, fiscal, and monetary policy, not to mention in foreign affairs. As previously noted, during the height of the 1958 recession, he bluntly accused the Republican administration of mismanaging the national debt and of misusing its power over the money supply to the detriment of the general welfare. As he spoke about these matters prior to the National Democratic Convention in early 1960, his Broadcast Pioneers speech in Chicago was not untypical: "It seems that when too much power...become[s] concentrated in a few hands, the people have to find a means to protect themselves," and that in a nation "like ours," he asserted, "remedies can be found without bloodshed."[35] Just as he had been provoked by Eisenhower's betrayal of bipartisanship in foreign affairs, so he became incensed by the failure of the administration to address the issues behind the recession. As he noted earlier, the reason for recession and the basic cause of Republican failure to maintain prosperity was due to its "high interest" or "tight money policy." Tight money, as he said on that occasion, "does not mean that the Government is being economical or frugal in spending its...money. It means that the Government is making it harder for its citizens to borrow money at the banks." There is nothing mysterious about that policy, Truman emphasized. "It is simply a way of using the mighty powers of public agencies to redistribute the national income in the wrong direction." As his former chairman of the Council of Economic Advisers, Leon Keyserling, put it: "From time immemorial, our economic philosophy has been that the economic tree should be watered at the bottom, not at the top."[36]

Like Roosevelt before him, Truman regarded the Democratic Party as "synonymous" with the American People and thus with the welfare of the nation. The Democratic Party, as he confided to Senator Joseph Clark of Pennsylvania in early 1960, has been the "only political party…that has the ordinary man's interest in its concept of what government is for," and that this has been the case since the early nineteenth century, and in this century in Wilson's presidency and in Franklin Roosevelt's "without reservation."[37] Some months later, he again emphasized this point in linking party and nation with the presidency in his letter to Symington: "My interest…is to make certain that we do not have a continuation of the present situation in government," suggesting that one way of meeting the situation would be "by passing legislation which will show the people plainly that the Democratic Party is for them and not for special interests."[38]

Truman's strategy in 1960, like some democratic codebook, was not dissimilar from his 1956 strategy, though commentators at the time seem not to have recognized this fact. Hence, in his news conference on 2 July 1960 in which he announced that he would resign as a delegate from the National Democratic Convention, he did so because he had wanted the convention to be open and he feared a "prearranged affair," and because he wanted a united party, not a divided one. Hence his direct question to Senator John Kennedy: "are you certain that you're quite ready for the country or the country is ready for you…in January, 1961?"[39] Mindful that Senator Kennedy, as well as Al Smith, were also Catholic, Truman believed that Kennedy might be too young to be the party's candidate, who, at forty-three, was sixteen years younger than Senator Symington, Truman's only presidential choice. Still, the overriding issue for Truman remained what it had always been: to nominate someone "who can be elected…on a platform that is for the welfare and benefit of the whole nation." In short, as Truman had noted in a prepared speech before the Executives Club in Chicago in May 1960, the Democratic candidate must be beholden to the general welfare at home, and be able to be "the leader of the free world."[40]

An issue, finally, that brought the Democratic leadership into line behind the party's nominees, Senators Kennedy and Johnson, was forthrightly expressed by Senator William Fulbright in his letter to Truman in early 1960. "The future looks mighty dark if we don't beat Nixon," he wrote on 16 March, a thought expressing Truman's own, and who, in comparing Nixon to Aaron Burr, also remembered "how close Jefferson came to losing the election in 1800" to Burr.[41]

The campaign that followed was all the more remarkable for the enthusiasm it rekindled in the former president, who had turned seventy-six in May 1960; still, it was the accumulated grievances of the previous eight years that helped rekindle the Truman spirit of old. Indeed, Senator Kennedy had been much taken by Truman's "personal guidance" and "private comments" on his visit to the Truman Library that summer, with the senator thanking him by letter on 29 August, and adding that he looked "forward to our common effort for the Democratic Party" in the fall.

In what would thus become a real political fight for the presidency, Truman planned to deliver at least seventeen or eighteen campaign speeches, especially in the South. It had been as if Mr. Truman had never left the White House, with former aides again helping with his speeches, particularly "Charlie" Murphy, and David H. Stowe, the latter traveling some 20,000 miles through nineteen states with the former president.[43]

Truman had thus set for himself a grueling schedule of speeches—he liked to call them lectures—in an effort to win back the presidency for the Democratic Party. Reminiscent of his 1948 campaign, his schedule of speaking engagements began in Spencer, Iowa, on 8 October. From there he traveled to Texas to make appearances in Texarkana, San Antonio, and Waco on 10-11 October. From there he went to Raleigh, Wilson, and Nashville, North Carolina, and thence to Abingdon, Virginia, on the 15th. On the 20th, he returned to Kansas City, after which he again traveled south to Jackson, Tennessee, including a stopover in Sikeston, Missouri, before going on to Mississippi, Alabama, and Louisiana.[44] On 9 October, the day after his speech in Spencer, Iowa, fittingly titled "Modern Agricultural History," Truman wrote his former secretary of state a long and optimistic letter: "I had a wonderful farm meeting in Iowa yesterday," and "was overwhelmed. If the Waco, Texas, religious meeting turns out all right I think we will then be on the road." If there was any anxiety in his letter, it was not apparent, except for his reference to Kennedy's Republican rival, Richard Nixon. "I certainly do appreciate the trouble you have gone…to give the facts and figures on Nixon. He is a dangerous man," adding that, "Never has there been one like him so close to the Presidency."[45]

Like his letters during this period, Truman's campaign speeches in 1960 were among the best of his post-White House years. At Baton Rouge, for instance, enroute to Abbeyville on the last leg of his second southern speech tour, Abbeyville's mayor had told him that the crowd had been the "biggest" he had ever seen. And once in Abbeyville Truman roused the audience with his lecture on the subject of "Political Campaign Tactics," subtitled "The Republicans Will Do Anything to Win an Election." The speech was a fighting exposé of Republican Party inaction on farm policy, social security, and foreign policy. On foreign policy, for example, in noting that Republican leaders suggest that the opposition "is serving…the 'cause of surrender,'" Truman stated that it is the Republicans who should be brought to account for "the most disgraceful surrender in our history…while Nixon…was Vice-President," in permitting "the forces of Communism to establish a new base in Cuba…90 miles from the shores of the United States."[46] In the same vein, his speech unmasked Republican Party tactics on farm policy and the Social Security program.

Returning to Kansas City from Louisiana, Truman continued on his speechmaking tour, traveling to Tacoma, Reno, and Oakland in late October. Reminiscing on his return to Kansas City on 26 October, Truman's optimism had been undiminished, as reflected in his letter to the governor of Louisiana, telling of meeting Kennedy there and displaying his excitement that the crowd at one of the shopping centers called "Truman Corners" had numbered some 50,000 people. Included in that letter was the hopeful phrase: "we are on the road to recovery and...ought to win this election."[47]

Without help, in fact, it seems unlikely that the young senator from Massachusetts could have won that election, as Truman thought, and as his daughter likewise believed. Truman himself had been surprised that the margin of victory had been so narrow: 49.7 percent to 49.5 percent of the popular votes cast, and 309 electoral college votes to 219.[48]

Even so, despite Kennedy's narrow victory, Truman believed that that fact has been of little importance historically. "Lest we forget," he added, "two of our greatest Presidents were elected for their first terms by a minority of the popular votes, although they had a majority of the electoral votes"—namely, Abraham Lincoln and Woodrow Wilson.[49] Narrow as Kennedy's victory had been, expressions of relief among the party's leaders at the outcome had been widely shared. Harriman, for example, in expressing great relief over the November election, wrote to Truman that the president-elect "should follow your example by using Republicans in bipartisan programs," but that the narrow victory, he believed, should not "lead him to appease the Republican leadership."[50] For Truman, likewise, the victory of the Democratic Party was reason enough to be hopeful about the future of American democracy, and the bipartisan approach in foreign affairs, so long as the president, as Harriman noted, did not yield to appeasement of his political opponents.[51] Similarly, though he maintained reservations about Kennedy's political maturity, and thus about his ability to make decisions, Truman remained hopeful that the new president would come to make a successful chief executive in the Jeffersonian-Jacksonian tradition.

There were, to be sure, sound reasons for such hopefulness. During the period between administrations, the president-elect had been aided during the transition by Clark Clifford, a Truman aide from 1946 to 1950, and Richard Neustadt, who had also served on Truman's White House staff. So, too, had the DAC, which had served as a strategic arm of the National Democratic

Committee, in providing Kennedy with ideas and timely reports, not to mention personnel for filling important governmental positions with former Truman administration officials. Murphy, for instance, a key figure on the DAC's administrative committee, became undersecretary in the Department of Agriculture. In all, more than thirty former Advisory Council and committee members of the council came to fill important administrative positions in the new administration, including former officials closely identified with foreign policy in the Truman era. Representative were George F. Kennan, who became Kennedy's ambassador to Yugoslavia; Harriman, who became assistant secretary of state for Far Eastern Affairs; Dean Rusk, who became secretary of state; Finletter, who was appointed ambassador to NATO; and James Webb, who headed the National Space and Aeronautics Administration, among others.[52]

To the extent that he could also, Truman wanted to be helpful to the new president. Indeed, the notion that the "Truman-Kennedy relationship never really warmed up" does not dovetail with the facts. As in the campaign, so President Kennedy's "enjoyment of their subsequent talks in the White House, were unbounded," as Theodore Sorensen, Kennedy's special counsel, would later write.[53]

Generally, despite ups and downs, Sorensen's conclusion accord with the known facts. Thus, writing to President Kennedy on 24 January, though he confessed that it had been the "first time" he had been invited to the White House in eight years, Truman emphasized, as he had earlier, that he wanted Kennedy's "administration to be most successful." Earlier, too, in his letter of reply on 3 January to the inaugural invitation, he wrote: "As President...you can tell me what you want me to do and I will be glad to do it." Again and again, Truman would remind the president that whenever he could be of "use in a constructive manner..., all you have to do is whisper...," as he confided to him early in 1962. Occasionally, when he thought it prudent to reinforce policy, Truman did not hesitate to remind President Kennedy that his no appeasement policy was entirely correct, when it concerned the opposition party. Typical in this vein was his letter to President Kennedy on 28 June 1962: "It looks as if the [Republicans] haven't changed a bit since 1936. President Roosevelt had his troubles with them—so did I," adding: "Don't let 'em tell you what to do. You tell them…Your suggestions for the public welfare, in my opinion, are correct."[54]

Truman's most useful role, it turns out, as an adviser to President Kennedy, may have been in the field of disarmament. Ralph Lapp, the former "Met Lab" physicist (named after the Metallurgical Laboratory involved in the atomic bomb project at the University of Chicago), tells of how former President Truman had interacted with scientists, senators, governors, and big city mayors in helping to convert some good ideas into political realities, most notable among these being "the concept of a National Peace Agency as a positive force for promoting arms control." Though the Advisory Committee on Science and Technology of the Democratic Advisory Council came up with the idea, a series of political steps were required to transform the concept of a "Peace Agency" into what became the Arms Control and Disarmament Agency. Viewed as a necessary measure in counteracting the dominance of the Pentagon—arguably another problem the Eisenhower administration failed to meet head-on—the new agency fell far short of such expectations.[55] Still, the Arms Control Agency did help to clarify the issues, and to that extent helped to change senators' minds in voting to support the treaty banning nuclear weapons tests between the U.S. and the Soviet Union in 1963.[56]

Accordingly, when President Kennedy invited Truman's input involving the "Nuclear Test Ban" agreement, banning nuclear tests in the atmosphere, in outer space, and under water, Truman assured the president, "after having read the text with care," that he had "no hesitancy about going along with the general sense of it." Writing again shortly afterward, Truman notified President Kennedy that he had written to Senator Fulbright, commending its approval, and that he "would be glad to make any statement" before the Senate Committee on Foreign Affairs, if "that would help in the ratification of the Treaty…" Characteristically, he concluded by saying that he was "exceedingly anxious to help in any way…for your welfare and benefit in 1964 …"[57]

Looking back, the former president felt assured—believed, in fact—that the Democratic Party must stand on its record in domestic as in foreign affairs, and that if it did, the party could more wisely reach decisions, based on that record, to benefit the general welfare. By contrast, the Eisenhower record in domestic and foreign affairs had reconfirmed Truman's view of the Republican Party, which, with few exceptions, he counted as favoring not the general welfare but "special interests."

CHAPTER VI: KEEPING THE NATION STRONG

FOREIGN POLICY AND NATIONAL SECURITY

In general, Truman's approach to foreign policy had rested on the two principles of bipartisanship and collective security in order to ensure that the respective parties and people remained united on issues affecting the nation's welfare and security, and, as expressed as the time of the formation of NATO, in order to serve "notice to the Soviet Union that imperialistic adventures in Europe would not be tolerated." So, in the fall of 1953, he spoke in defense of these principles at a gathering in New York by invoking U.S. support of NATO, the RIO Pact of 1947, and the "Pacific alliances," being U.S. support of its defensive agreements with Japan, the Philippines, and the ANZUS Treaty (with Australia and New Zealand).[1] These same principles were implicit in the Mutual Security Act of 1951, a measure that envisioned a modicum of economic and military assistance to Middle East, African, and Asian nations, though the Truman administration had adamantly refused to entertain any collective security agreements with countries on the Asian mainland.[2]

The following year, in a speech at the Municipal Auditorium in Kansas City, the former president again stressed the importance of these principles in criticizing their mishandling by the administration, adding that in less than two years "many of our friends and allies have lost confidence in the stability of American foreign policy." Truman, in fact, attributed the loss of confidence in U.S. diplomacy to the ascendency of extremist elements within the Republican Party. He thus felt that the problems in U.S. diplomacy stemmed from these same extremist elements: "isolationalists who would turn their backs on the United Nations," and who want "to pass a Constitutional amendment (the Bricker Amendment) to cripple the ability of the President to conduct foreign affairs," and those "who would push us into intervention in China, even at the risk of another world war."[3] Acheson, too, had early questioned the administration's handling of foreign policy, especially as to the Soviet Union. In July 1953, for instance, he confided to Truman that "1953 has much in common with 1949," despite Stalin's passing earlier that year, and that Eisenhower ought to hold a four-power meeting in order to smoke out the Russians and strengthen his hand at home by discrediting "the demagogic isolationist wing of the Republican Party which wishes to…separate us from our allies."[4]

However promising his approach, Acheson's agenda found no counterpart to the administration's own. Instead, Eisenhower and Dulles preferred to engage in abstract talk about "falling dominoes" and its alleged remedy, a security treaty to thwart such an outcome—states succumbing to communism as China had—on the Asian mainland. In fact, only a week after the signing of the armistice in Korea, President Eisenhower, in addressing a Conference of Governors' in Seattle, first advanced what later became known as the "domino theory." In that address, though oddly downgraded as being unimportant, he made reference to the fact that if Indochina fell, "several things [would] happen right away. The Malayan peninsula…would be scarcely defensible—and tin and tungsten that we so greatly value from that area would cease coming." As a result, "India would be outflanked" and Burma would be "weakened," an eventuality, he noted, that would be "very ominous for the United States"; hence the reason for the French forces being there to maintain control.[5] Thereafter, on 7 April 1954, only a month before the fall of Dien Bien Phu—the French defeat in North Vietnam—Eisenhower again talked about the area's strategic importance. Giving credence to the notion of what he called the "falling domino principle," he speculated that if one country fell under communist rule, the outcome would mark the "beginning of a disintegration that would have the most profound influences." Recalling that press conference some years later, Eisenhower's chief aide wrote that Indochina's fall was viewed as leading to the loss of Burma, Thailand, Malaya, and Indonesia, and threatening in turn Australia, New Zealand, the Philippines, and Japan.[6] In reality, however, such speculation was not the only reason behind Eisenhower's so-called "domino principle."

Briefly, Eisenhower's apparent reason for highlighting the notion about falling dominoes had been to reinforce "Dulles' effort" to obtain bipartisan support for an Asian security treaty that the Truman administration had previously opposed. As Sherman Adams, Eisenhower's aide, remembered it: the secretary of state had lobbied for some "six months" prior to the SEATO (Southeast Asian Treaty Organization) Conference in 1954, irrespective of the Geneva Conference of 1954 convened to settle the issues involved, at which time "Dulles held more than ninety meetings with Congressional leaders of both parties."[7]

Dean Rusk, for one, had regarded the SEATO Treaty as a mistake. Assistant secretary of state for Far Eastern Affairs in the Truman administration, he expressed amazement that the Senate did not debate the SEATO Treaty as they had the Atlantic Alliance, as President Truman thought that the U.S. "should stay offshore, largely because of our own experience in Asia and the experience of colonial powers before, during, and after the war [World Warr II]." Truman, in short, had viewed it as "unwise to involve the United States in security treaties on the Asian mainland."[8]

Although modeled on NATO, SEATO had no organization, and lacked NATO's teeth. Article IV had skirted the issue about an armed attack on one nation as being an armed attack on all—the language of NATO. Instead, it said that in the event of an armed attack in the treaty area, Southeast Asia and the Southwest Pacific, each party "will in that event act to meet the common danger in accordance with its constitutional processes." Thus, despite SEATO's apparent deficiencies in providing any real security in a collective sense, it opened the door to the direct use of military force in checking such aggression. In this way, then, did the Eisenhower-Dulles foreign policy break with "the limited and historically defined objectives" of the Truman administration by becoming unlimited, and open-ended? As Dulles himself declared: "Our foreign policy can best be explained by extending to the whole world the words of the Preamble to the Constitution…"[9]

Henceforth, the issue was not where the SEATO Treaty might lead U.S. policymakers, but where the new Eisenhower-Dulles interventionist policy toward Asia, or domino principle, might lead.[10] And so, because of the continued Chinese communist provocations against the offshore islands of Quemoy and Matsu, the dangers posed by such a policy became impossible to ignore.[11]

Indeed, one of the first members of the Senate Foreign Relations Committee to raise the issue was Oregon's senator, Wayne Morse. Only a month after the Senate's approval of the SEATO Treaty, in March 1955, Morse confided to Truman that he had "absolutely no confidence in the machinations of one John Foster Dulles...and the other spokesmen for the Administration, who seem to be directing Asiatic policy these days." He added that in going about the country, he found "a growing recognition of the great difference in principles between your Asiatic policies and the Asiatic policy of the present Administration." Specifically, the Chinese communist leaders were apparently using the offshore islands as bait, as the former UNRRA (United Nations Relief and Rehabilitation Administration) director in China, Ben Kizer, who had worked with Chou En-lai, informed Morse. Truman's Senate conferee concluded by saying that he was "at a loss to understand why the Administration does not make clear that we will defend Formosa to the hilt, but that we are not willing...to defend Quemoy and Matsu."[12]

It was to be some three years later, however, before Eisenhower's Asian policy prompted Mr. Truman to address the subject in one of his articles for the North American Newspaper Alliance. Previously, Acheson and Truman had discussed the administration's Asian policy and the offshore islands of Quemoy and Matsu, especially Quemoy, which the Nationalist government on Formosa (Taiwan) had been allowed to garrison since 1953. Consistent with their agreement that this action had been as "fraudulent"as it had been "wrong" in permitting Chiang Kai-shek's "army on Quemoy to make a pretense at invasion" had been their apparent agreement on the policy behind it; namely, the so-called domino theory.[13]

Only ten days before Truman's article appeared in the *New York Times* on 14 September 1958, Dulles journeyed to Newport, Rhode Island, where Eisenhower was vacationing. What he took with him for discussion with the president, since termed the "Newport Memorandum," represented a "classic exposition" of the so-called domino theory. As the theory had earlier been applied to the fall of Indochina, and, as a result, to all of Southeast Asia, so the Newport Memorandum applied the theory to the "loss or surrender" of Quemoy in the Formosa Strait, some fifteen miles from China's Amoy island harbor. According to the memorandum, the loss of Quemoy would threaten the anti-communist government on Formosa, and in turn the entire "insular positions" of the Western Pacific and Southeast Asia: Japan, the Philippines, Thailand, Laos, Cambodia, and Vietnam, as well as Indonesia, Malaya, and Burma.[14]

In contrast to the previously agreed position taken by Truman and Acheson on the administration's Asian policy, Truman's article on Quemoy had virtually sided with the administration's almost primitive stand on the issue of the offshore islands. In consequence, a "somewhat bewildered" Acheson wrote the former president on 16 September: "Please don't be hooked on one of those 'my country right or wrong' gambits. In this way," Acheson averred, Dulles "can always drive us like steers to the slaughter pens."[15] And in a follow up letter, he wrote a long refutation of the domino theory, though he never mentioned it by name. Acheson, in fact, focused on the "central point," and about which they had earlier agreed to oppose: the assertion that "Whenever and wherever we are challenged by the Communists…we must meet that challenge. Certainly," he added, "you did not want to fight in Hungary," and that, "This opposition to Russia is a dangerous business which requires lots of sense and coolness in making decisions of where and how."[16]

Suffice to record that while Truman and his former secretary of state had "rather bad luck in getting on opposite sides of foreign policy questions," as Acheson noted in the case of China's offshore islands, on Berlin, on Cuba, and on Asia generally, they were usually in agreement.[17]

AFTER 1958

After six years then, with the dubious exception of Republican strategy involving the SEATO Treaty, the perceived failure to invite bipartisan consultations on foreign policy matters had largely soured Truman on the administration's handling of foreign affairs during the last two years of Eisenhower's presidency. As in his letter of 14 October 1958, Truman informed Acheson that in his travels around the country and in "listening to what people have to say," he found the citizenry to be "entirely confused by the procedure of the present administration on foreign policy." He added that "if we...could find out...the foreign policy of the present administration...," we could decide whether we wanted "to support it or not," concluding: "I repeat, the bipartisan foreign policy has never been in existence since you and I left the White House."[18]

Truman's renewed criticism of the administration on foreign policy grounds clearly raised questions about Eisenhower's priorities involving the national interest, about the utilization of U.S. intelligence abroad, and about the administration's stand on the Mutual Security Program. Thus, in his testimony before the House Committee on Foreign Affairs to amend the Mutual Security Act in early 1959, Truman recalled that the program had been a bipartisan one, that it had been conducive to the nation's welfare, that its emphasis should be on "the economic aspects" rather than on military assistance, and that it ought to be conceived, much as the Marshall Plan, as a four or five-year program. And his support of the program had been for the best reasons: the national interest and common defense against aggression and for humanitarian reasons as exemplified by the program's Development Loan fund. Similarly, though he emphasized the importance of the Loan Fund through the improvement of "living standards and the health and welfare of the nations" involved, he did not overlook "the military aspects of the program." As he saw it, to be sure, the president had a clear duty to investigate the program in making decisions to render such assistance.[19] And while he refrained from mentioning Cuba by name, as with other relevant political issues in these hearings, he said that he would wait until the 1960 campaign before commenting further. Interesting, too, was the fact that Truman alluded to the Eightieth Congress and the opposition's support for his foreign policy program then, though he did not mention the two senators who had been indispensable for their bipartisan support in 1947-48: Arthur Vandenberg and Robert Taft, two senators he had mentioned earlier as "Great Senators" in contributing to the general welfare (education) and the national interest (bipartisanship).[20]

The previous day, on 4 May 1959, Truman had also testified in hearings before the Senate's Judiciary Committee on a proposed amendment to the Constitution to repeal the Twenty-Second Amendment, a further issue with foreign policy and national security implications. As he had said on another occasion with equal force, though not before the Senate Judiciary Committee, he had doubted whether members of Congress who voted in favor of the amendment had read the "arguments...against such a procedure," as set forth in the debates of 1787 and in the *Federalist Papers*, about limiting the president's tenure to two full terms. Although referring to the Eightieth Congress and "the Roosevelt haters"—he did not mention that "all of the Republicans" and "some very right-wing Democrats" voted for the amendment—in selling the country on the idea, he pointed out that all the amendment did "was to make a 'lame duck' out of every second-term President for all time," and that in any future crisis the term limitation could prove to be "tragic" in its consequences for the nation's safety and the general welfare.[21]

Foreign policy issues continued to occupy his attention as the new decade opened, even if the issue of bipartisanship did not for the next several years. This was surely because the new Democratic administration would be called upon to address such problems that the Eisenhower administration had failed to resolve or even mention, as in the case of Vietnam.[22] As Malcolm Muggeridge, a distinguished British journalist, noted, after reading Sherman Adams' memoir of his years in the Eisenhower White House: "Adams refers to how they 'solved' various problems like Korea, etc. In fact, none of them solved," he recorded in his diary.[23]

In point of fact, such problems seemed myriad as the new decade opened: Cuba and Indochina, Berlin, nuclear fallout, the future of NATO, and overall relations with the Soviet Union. As Truman confided to Acheson not long after the Bay of Pigs fiasco in 1961: "As to Berlin and Laos and Indo-China and Cuba, we have problems and problems. May...God help us to solve them!"[24]

Unquestionably, the disastrous outcome of invading Cuba in April 1961 by CIA-trained Cuban insurgents had been a wrenching defeat for the new and inexperienced chief executive. In retrospect, however, that Kennedy had failed to meet the Soviet challenge seems odd, although he had been badly advised both by his U.N. ambassador, Adlai Stevenson, and by his secretary of state, Dean Rusk. In fact, Acheson would later lament that he had recommended Rusk to the new president in a letter to his former "boss," saying that Rusk "had been a good assistant," but that "as number one he has been no good at all."[25]

And so, in the aftermath of the Bay of Pigs debacle, Vice President Johnson was given the task of talking with Truman about "some of the background and circumstances of the Cuban episode," while Rusk took the occasion to write the former president about what went wrong. "Our information on two key points proved to be seriously wrong," he confided to Truman on 25 April. The two points had concerned "the readiness or ability of the Cuban people to rise against Castro and the quantity and types of Soviet arms already in the island." Truman replied two days later saying that he was glad "to have the information," and that he wanted "to be helpful in anything that will make the administration run smoother..."[26] Notwithstanding, also, Rusk's assurances to Truman that the administration was taking its "lessons seriously," the failure of the Cuban venture to topple Castro would transform Soviet estimates of American resolve and increase their "foothold in Cuba," including the eventual decision to deliver nuclear missiles to Castro the following year.[27]

Rightly or wrongly, Mr. Truman put part of the blame for the failure of the Bay of Pigs venture on the Central Intelligence Agency. Truman's former National Security Council aide, Sidney W. Souers, who served as the CIA's first director by Executive Order in 1947, apparently thought likewise. "Allen Dulles caused the C.I.A. to wander far from the original goal established by you," Souers wrote, citing its involvement in *coup d'état's* "in smaller countries around the globe." As to the failed Bay of Pigs operation, he added: "As bad as that was, it was worse to try to conduct a 'war'...with a handful of men and without air cover."[28]

Although the Cuban missile crisis of 1962 proved to be anticlimactic, it did not seem so at the time. Nikita Khrushchev, the Soviet premier, who wanted to find out for himself if the new president was as "vulnerable" as he appeared in the light of the failed Cuban venture, met with President Kennedy in Vienna two months later, in June 1961. To the horror of foreign service officers who read the transcript of the Kennedy-Khrushchev conversations, it was apparent that Kennedy "*had* been browbeaten by Khrushchev"—thus reinforcing his earlier impression of the American president. "I know for certain," Khrushchev boasted after the talks, "that Kennedy doesn't have a strong backbone nor, generally speaking, does he have the courage to stand up to a serious challenge." Thus was the decision made to risk gaining an "almost instant nuclear advantage by installing missiles in Cuba only ninety miles from the United States."[29]

That the Soviet regime, and Khrushchev in particular, would undertake such a clandestine operation could not have greatly surprised former President Truman. He had only conveyed to President Kennedy his attitude toward the Communists, when, in a visit to the White House, he had characterized them as "all crazy."[30] Truman, in fact, had been in the midst of a campaign to help reelect Democrats to Congress when the missile crisis broke, forcing him to cancel his speaking engagements that fall. Truman, however, did agree to an interview with the Canadian Broadcasting Company on 27 October, the day before the crisis ended with Khrushchev's abandonment of the missile deployment sites on Cuban soil. Noting that he had "had to deal with Russian duplicity and truculence through all the years" of his own administration, when Soviet propaganda kept "putting out a steady barrage proclaiming peaceful intentions," while preparing for war, he recalled such crises, as instanced in Berlin, "when they attempted to *freeze* and *starve*" the city "into surrender, and force former allies out of that part of Germany in violation of our agreement." The airlift, though "a costly and hazardous task," worked, adding that although "they have established a missile bridgehead in Cuba," the Soviets will be stopped there too.[31]

On the following day, 28 October, as Khrushchev yielded and "agreed to dismantle and withdraw the missiles under adequate supervision and inspection," President Kennedy placed telephone calls to former presidents Truman and Eisenhower," notifying them of the Soviet decision to withdraw its missiles from Cuba. Gladdened by the end of the crisis lasting only "thirteen days," as Truman had known longer ones as president, he wrote that he looked forward to the day when Cuba would again be free, as he felt sure, "sooner or later...will happen."[32]

Ironically, while Kennedy's handling of the missile crisis had ended as Truman predicted, a further foreign policy issue remained to be resolved: the issue of continued U.S. aid to South Vietnam and the related issue of U.S. policy toward Asia.

Suffice to note that the so-called domino theory—starting with the Eisenhower administration and to some extent during the Kennedy years—again played a part. But so had another pernicious factor in impeding the reformulation of U.S. policy toward Vietnam between 1960 and 1964; namely, the legend that the U.S. had "lost China to the Communists." Last, despite the reversal in Soviet policy towards the PRC and Moscow's interest in North Vietnam's efforts "to impede...Chinese (Communist) hegemony in Southeast Asia" after 1959, and despite U.S. intelligence estimators who recognized the importance of this key change in Soviet policy, "U.S. policy never took cognizance of it." In short, the failure to reformulate U.S. policy toward Vietnam under Kennedy's successor had been painfully apparent to the intelligence estimators: to render increased aid to South Vietnam would turn "a low-level...civil war into a modern war," would risk making "North Vietnam a formidable military power," because of Soviet aid to Hanoi after 1959, and risk increased U.S. involvement in an area nonvital to the U.S. but of advantage to Soviet Third World interests in Asia and beyond.[33]

The thought that current intelligence estimates should not be fully taken into account in foreign policy-making ran counter to everything Truman had had in mind when he established the Central Intelligence Agency and the National Security Council (NSC). So Souers himself testified before a Senate Subcommittee on how the NSC can best function as an advisory body to the president, having served as the first executive secretary of the NSC from 1947 to 1950: "I think the President should be consistently [aided] by his Special Assistant," he testified, since that assistant "keeps in close touch with the departments as they are developing their policy views."[34] And Truman, who fathered the CIA and NSC, had been no less emphatic: "I don't know what the program of the present occupant of the White House is," he confided to Senator Morse some months after the Cuban missile crisis, "but...if he doesn't know what is going on from every angle there is no way for him to carry on a foreign policy."[35]

Secondly, though the change in Sino-Soviet relations ought to have resulted in a comparable shift in U.S. Asian policy, including Vietnam policy, such a shift ought to have become imperative after the Soviet reversal toward China became public in 1964.[36] Thirdly, had not, also, another kind of change—and one of uncertainty—opened the decade of the 1960s as the 1950s (1953-63) ended with the abrupt passing of the Kennedy administration in November 1963? Truman, for example, while grievously shaken by Kennedy's assassination, had been looking forward to President Kennedy's visit to Kansas City on 30 January 1964 "to celebrate the 25th Anniversary of the March of Dimes and the Birthday of President Roosevelt." So he wrote to Senator Symington, only a few days after Kennedy's tragic death; he thought the 30 January meeting should be called off "unless we can make it a Presidential Memorial meeting for President Kennedy." Again, as he noted in his letter of 26 November: "I am cancelling all of my engagements, political or otherwise, between now and the first of January and then we will start anew."[37]

A new start, however, was not to be made in foreign and national security affairs, as Truman soon found himself writing letters of admonition. "Please excuse my impertinence," he confided to the new president. "I think you are doing too much too often. You'll find, as I did, that most of the so-called emergencies will...settle themselves." There were also voices of moderation and reason inside the Johnson White House, but such voices were not to prevail when it came to the question of increased U.S. involved in Vietnam. George Reedy, for instance, Johnson's special assistant for speechwriting and press relations when Johnson became vice president in 1961, provides a case in point. Reedy thought—was sure, in fact—that it would have been relatively easy for President Johnson "to disengage from Vietnam" in 1964, given the fact that the "war had made very little impression upon the American people" in comparison to other issues "on the front burner."[38] At such moments of transition, Truman's own *Memoirs* provided some guidance, when he wrote: "From my reading of American history, I knew there was no cut-and-dried answer...of what obligations a President...had in regard to the program of his predecessor," except for the "basic policy...that the country should be operated for the benefit of all the people." Even Truman's later account, published in 1960, provided some useful advise in presidential decision-making. Everyone "makes mistakes," the former president acknowledged in his chapter entitled "Spot Decisions," adding that he "always tried to remedy the mistake by making another decision."[39]

Yet President Johnson had been incapable of admitting error—had never confessed to error "in his entire life"—according to his press secretary, George Reedy. Johnson, Reedy even noted, believed "that another Communist victory on the mainland of Asia"—the "lost China" legend—"could open up another 'era of McCarthyism.'" And Johnson seemed to view the Vietnam

War "as part of the national presidential heritage"; that is, in "carrying on what three Presidents before him had supported…"[40] Lastly, his demonstrable failure to reexamine U.S. Asian policy had troubled the former president, despite some earlier evidence to the contrary.

Truman, who turned eighty in May 1964, had done all that he could to help the Democratic Party to regain the White House, but he was no longer able to play an active part as he had in 1960. Nor was he able to attend the Democratic National Convention in August 1964, having explained—as on another occasion earlier that year—that he was at work on a book he hoped to write on "each…of our Presidents."[41] When, alas, he fell and broke his glasses, "and cracked a couple of ribs" nearly two months later, it was not until November that he was able to return to his office at the Truman Library. Writing about his fateful fall to Mrs. Warren Austin that November, the wife of his former U.N. ambassador, he recalled how "highly interested" he had been in Kennedy's "welfare." As for President Johnson, he added, "I am sure he won't let us down."[42]

It was with difficulty, then, that Truman found himself having to reply to queries concerning his views on Vietnam early the following year. His effort, in fact, resulted in a heavily edited article, "Truman Asks Patience in South Vietnam," which appeared in the *Kansas City Star* on 24 January 1965. The article contained several key paragraphs that ought to be of much interest to historians and political scientists. In one of these he compared the conflict in South Vietnam to the problem that confronted the Greek nation after World War II. It was significant because President Johnson had tried to use this same argument in selling the Vietnam conflict, but which even "his strongest supporters" would not buy. "The differences between Greece"—a Western nation and the "cradle of Western civilization"—and Vietnam—a non-Western, "Buddhist enclave—were too striking for the comparison to withstand much inspection," as Reedy recorded in his *Memoir*. Another paragraph in Truman's article was equally significant, because it went to the heart of the problem of policy without the input of the intelligence estimators, since Mr. Truman wrote the article without benefit of such information. After referring to the abandonment of Vietnam by France, he went on to note that a "new colonial power" had taken its place; namely, "Communist China," which "became interested in absorbing all of Vietnam in the Communist bloc..."[43]

Doubtless, as this article was written in January 1965, what he wrote then would have been applicable before the "break-up of the Communist monolith" in 1960-61, but not afterward. What he had written, therefore, ought to have stirred the Johnson administration into action because of the disintegration of the Communist bloc some four or five years before. What followed, consequently, was not any failure of Truman's but the failure of presidential policy on Lyndon Johnson's "watch." Thus, in reply to Senator Symington's anxiety-ridden letter on the Vietnam War of 9 March 1967, more than two years later, Truman responded as well as he could: "Every administration has problems peculiar to a period, and it has to deal with them in its own way."[44]

Earlier, in criticism of Eisenhower's interventionist Asian policies, the former president had warned of its dangers to national unity in keeping the nation strong; and so that warning had again become applicable more than a decade later, and even more transparent in 1967.

On his first European trip since 1945, President Harry S. Truman visits with F. Forlati in May 1956 in San Marco Square, Venice, Italy. (Harry S. Truman Library)

President Truman, on the occasion of his visit to Key West, with Mrs. Truman, in 1968. (U.S. Navy photo)

President Truman with the Raytown Debate team, 6 February 1958. (Kansas City Star Co.)

PART III

THE BETTER WORLD—A CONTINUING QUEST

CHAPTER VII: AMBASSADOR OF GOOD WILL
(1956-64)

FIRST EUROPEAN TRIP SINCE 1945

Three years after the Trumans had visited Hawaii "to get a little rest and sunshine," they embarked on another journey abroad by traveling to the European continent and from there to England. The occasion had been a long-delayed one, to receive an honorary degree from Oxford in 1953. Unable to accept the invitation then, it was renewed in 1954; postponed again because of a gall bladder operation, it was renewed in 1955, and accepted for the following June.

Coincidentally, plans for the trip nearly coincided with the marriage of their daughter, Margaret, who informed her father "that he was going to have a newspaperman for a son-in-law." When a month later, her future husband, Clifton Daniel of the *New York Times*, met her father for the first time—Daniel had recently returned from the Soviet Union "with a bad case of ulcers"—he could drink only milk and not spirits. Margaret enjoyed watching her father's reaction: "A newspaperman and he drinks milk!" Yet Margaret, her father later recorded, "had found a grand man," and on 21 April 1956 the marriage took place "to the satisfaction" of all "and apparently the entire nation."[1]

Earlier, Truman had declined to travel abroad, because he had been "tied up," as he said, "with [his] memoirs." But in 1956, he was free at last from his commitment to Time-Life, Inc., as the last volume of his *Memoirs* was then being published. Interestingly, Daniel Longwell, editor of *Life* magazine, had written to Churchill's longtime physician, Lord Moran, saying that he ought to meet Truman when he arrives in England, and adding: "I am afraid he...does not realize the importance of his trip abroad, and how well he is thought of there," and what "elaborate arrangements may have been made for him."[2] Churchill, moreover, had been pleased to learn of Truman's acceptance of the Oxford invitation, and expressed the hope that he would not fail to join him for a quiet dinner on that occasion. The two men had not seen one another since Truman's last year in the presidency.

Truman, for his part, replied later that month on 24 March, saying that "your invitation is a definite engagement and is most highly appreciated."[3]

Nonetheless, Truman was not unaware of the significance of his first European trip since 1945. Notably, he had asked Hillman, his literary aide, "to deliver a personal message" to King Paul of Greece well beforehand. Accordingly, on 10 March 1956, Truman's emissary was received by King Paul, who regretfully conveyed Mr. Truman's reasons for not visiting Greece on his "planned visit to Europe" that spring and early summer. As Hillman told the king, he did not want his visit "to be made the object of international or domestic politics, and that until after the 1956 elections" he "could not venture into the area of the Middle East." Presumably, were he to visit Greece, he would have had to visit Turkey, as well as Israel. Through Hillman, Mr. Truman also wanted the king to know that all he wanted was "peace, especially for Greece, and that there was no reason for introducing any new elements of controversy...which might arise from [his] visit." Subsequently, following Hillman's report on Greece, on 24 March, Truman held a news conference, and explained his decision to "avoid the Middle East in his forthcoming tour because of unrest there," though he did not mention the main issue in the region then dividing some of NATO's allies—namely, the problem of Cyprus.[4]

There were, however, two related matters upon which the former president had been able to agree in advance of his seven-week trip. He agreed to write a series of ten articles for the New York *Journal-American* and King Features Snydicate. The articles he planned to write, based on diary notes he kept of that trip, and like most of his writing, were "remarkably frank" impressions of his journey from New York, ending only with his first visit to London.[5] He had also agreed to give his "impressions and conclusions" after his forty-nine-day trip in an off-the-record talk with members of the Council on Foreign Relations in New York, and publisher of the influential *Foreign Affairs* quarterly. Accepting in principle the council's invitation to meet informally with its membership, Truman so notified John J. McCloy, the council's board chairman, in his letter of 2 May. "As you may know," he concluded, "we sail from New York on May 11th and will not return...until July 4th. If you have the time...to call me at the Hotel Carlyle, perhaps we can come to some agreement before I leave."[6]

Accompanied by Stanley Woodward and his wife (Woodward served as Truman's Chief of Protocol in his presidential days, and later was his ambassador to Canada), the party duly arrived at the Carlyle, where Truman, who had just celebrated his seventy-second birthday in Kansas City on 8 May, was greeted with another birthday cake before boarding their ship, the *United States*, three days later. The scene, as he noted, was vastly different from 1945, eleven years before, when he boarded the U.S.S. *Augusta* enroute to Antwerp to attend the Potsdam Conference, adding that "This trip...will be a much more pleasant one."[7]

Arriving at the port city of Le Havre, France, on 16 May, the Trumans and Woodwards motored by "boat train" to Paris, and from there to Rome the following day. Arriving there on 18 May, they "received a tumultuous welcome at Rome's railroad terminal," where the Truman's were met by officials, reporters, and photographers. Subsequently, Truman told the reporters at a news conference that he had pressed for the establishment of U.S.-Vatican diplomatic relations when he was president, because "Such relations would help the peace of the world," saying too that he had "not received such a wonderful reception since [his return] to Washington" after the 1948 election.[8] Following a private audience with Pope Pius XII, the Trumans and Woodwards journeyed to Naples, and from there to Assisi, Florence, and Venice, before taking a train to Salzburg the following week.

One of his most memorable visits in the course of that week took place on the outskirts of Florence, where Truman met with the Christian humanist and art historian, Bernard Berenson, at his villa, "I Tatti." For Berenson—a Jewish convert to Christianity—it had also been a memorable visit. In his epochal diary, recorded the next day, Berenson wrote: "Truman and his wife lunched yesterday. Came at one and stayed till three. Both as natural, as unspoiled by high office as if he had got no further than alderman of Independence." Berenson added that in his long life—he was then ninety-two—he had "never met an individual" with whom he "so instantly felt at home." The former president "talked as if he had always known me," and willing "to touch on any subject, no matter how personal." Movingly, he concluded: "Now I feel more assured about America than in a long time. If the Truman miracle can still occur, we need not fear..."[9]

Not least, surely, the Truman miracle owed something to character and experience, and a facility for decision-making. As Leon Keyserling, former economic adviser in the Truman administration, pointed out, these characteristics were already present before "he got" to the presidency; hence, his decisiveness in rescuing postwar Europe also helps explain the enormous goodwill with which the former president was greeted. Indeed, an editorial in Rome's *Il Giornale D'Italia*, one of Italy's leading independent dailies, seemed to capture the significance of Truman's visit. The "Italian people have even greater reasons for appreciation and gratitude for President Truman" than his suggestion in 1945, over allied objections, "that Italy be admitted to the United Nations"; i.e., for "the generous and timely aid when everything had collapsed and the miracle of reconstruction and recovery seemed a dream."[10] Likewise, leaving Italy, especially Venice and its "art treasures and historical monuments" still unseen, made the visit all too short, Truman recorded in his diary. And in his letter to Senator Symington on 28 May, shortly before leaving for Salzburg, he wrote: "The Italian elections have been going on...and from the reception I have received in all the big cities...I almost believe I could be elected over here."[11]

The main purpose in journeying to Salzburg and nearby St. Jakob am Thurn, the Woodwards' European home, was to rest and prepare a speech to be delivered in England on the last leg of their trip. Actually, Truman would deliver two speeches there, one to be given at Oxford on 20 June, and his Pilgrims speech in London the following day. As Truman confided to his former

White House aide, "Charlie" Murphy, on 2 June: "We arrived in Salzburg last night to find your letter of May 21" with "the revised draft of the Pilgrims speech. I am sure," he added, "with a few personal interpolations, it will fit the bill exactly."[12]

The brief holiday near Salzburg had also been eventful, as Truman noted in a *Journal-American* article drafted there, especially in musical terms. "Salzburg was the birthplace and home of the great Mozart, the composer I most admire," he wrote. "The second thing was that in Salzburg I would be able to get a firsthand account of conditions behind the Iron Curtain," from "an account…of the brave men and women who have fled to freedom." As to the former, as Elise Kirk has pointed out, "Truman was in his glory" on his first post-presidential trip to Europe—especially in Salzburg. "He played part of Mozart's Sonata in A Major on the 250-year old organ at the Salzburg Cathedral, visited Mozart's home,…and was entertained at a concert of Mozart's music at the former palace of the archbishop of Salzburg." On 4 June, the next day, Truman summed up the events of that weekend in writing that he had "never attended a happier or pleasing musical event."[13] As to the latter, Truman observed that the Austrians were fortunate to have regained their freedom from Russian control, since treatment of their satellite states in Central and Eastern Europe compared, he thought, with "the teaching and example of Genghis Khan and Tamerlane."[14]

Apparently rested and enchanted by the "solid contentment" of Mozart's "town," the Trumans set out for Munich on 6 June, enroute to Paris and then to London on 18 June. In Paris, Truman was much interested to learn whether America's "European Allies were losing interest in the military side of NATO," and in talks with Frenchmen to learn whether the rank and file of the French people had "forgotten the American efforts in their behalf in both world wars." He was not to be disappointed, winding up his visit to France with a tour of NATO's military headquarters at nearby Rocquencourt, and for the first time seeing the organization's "headquarters that was established when he was President."[15] He was leaving Europe, as he wrote in one of his last *Journal-American* articles, with the definite impression of a people whose collective expressions of "friendship and gratitude" reflected such sentiments toward his country rather than himself. "It is difficult…to describe," he acknowledged, but he believed that it was so.[16]

In a real sense, as Woodward told the former president, "London is the last whistle stop." And so it was. On 20 June, Truman received the long-delayed and long-awaited honorary degree of Doctor of Civil Law from the University of Oxford. And on the following day, at the Pilgrims dinner in London, he was again honored by his British and Commonwealth admirers. Earl Attlee, for instance, described Mr. Truman's decision to defend South Korea as a "courageous" act, and largely responsible for the survival of the United Nations, while Australia's Prime Minister, Robert Menzies, hailed the former president as a "great man."[17]

At Oxford, Truman had recalled the struggle of nineteenth century man in his quest for individual and political freedom, but spoke of twentieth century man as still being denied these "inalienable" rights. "In short, we must declare…a new Magna Carta," and "a new Declaration of Independence," he said. "We must give every boy and girl, not just the rudiments of education, but [the] highest educational training from which they can profit," the full benefit of "medical advances," and "economic well-being and security." And in his Pilgrims dinner address, he reaffirmed not only the importance of the English language and the democratic way of life as the ties that bind the American nation but also as the ties that bind "our two countries."[18]

Before embarking on their homeward journey, the Trumans dined with the Churchills, immediate family members, and Lord Beaverbrook. It was an occasion, Truman wrote, that would long "be remembered and an experience never to be forgotten"; Churchill, he noted, even "remarked that it would be a great thing for the world if" he again became president. Beaverbrook had been equally sincere in telling the former president "that, on this European trip," he had "made the greatest ambassador of goodwill the U.S.A. had ever had here."[19]

AFTER 1956

The Trumans seven-nation tour and the reception accorded the ex-president had been unprecedented. Recalling his visit to Chartwell the previous month at Churchill's country home, Truman also thanked the former prime minister for sending the first volume of his *History of the English-Speaking Peoples*, adding: "The opportunity of talking with you there and seeing you at the Prime Minister's dinner were the highlights of our stay in England." Equally warmed by the reception they had been accorded throughout that trip, Truman still regarded, as he said, such expressions of gratitude and affection as showing "gratitude to the American people" than to any individual.[20]

Next to the heartwarming crowds, the Trumans had also been much impressed by Europe's cultural and historical antiquities. Their trip through southern Italy and the ruins of Pompei, something Truman had studied years before, had prompted anew his interest in "its people and the civilization of that time." They thus wished to return to Europe, but without the press and media attention being focused on their sightseeing plans and whether or not a second trip might have some "political or international implications." And so, when the Truman's returned to Europe in 1958, unlike their earlier trip, it was without any official reason for doing so. Accompanied by longtime friends, Samuel I. Rosenman and Mrs. Rosenman of New York, they departed for the Mediterranean aboard the American Export Liner *Independence* on 26 May 1958. Reaching Naples on 3 June, the former president declined to comment on the current "French crisis," saying only that they "would vacation on the Riviera as planned if the situation in France remained quiet." Happily, then, except for sightseeing through the Roman ruins of southern France, at Avignon, Nimes, and Arles, which was reported in the press, they were able largely to escape the questioning of reporters and the obligatory news conference, and simply enjoy "a vacation."[21]

Nevertheless, as the former president's party boarded an American ship at Cannes, Truman decided to issue a public statement stemming from the Sherman Adams scandal that had been in the press reports since the matter became public several weeks earlier. Until then, he had refused to comment on public affairs at home, because he had been on "foreign soil." Once aboard the U.S.S. *Constitution*, however, he used the Adams scandal to highlight what he described as the "bungling and failures" of Eisenhower's presidency: not just the "lack of ethics in the White House" but "the complete failure and disastrous results" of its foreign and domestic policies. "Were it not for the cushions built into the economy," the statement concluded, "we would be in as much trouble at home as we are abroad with our foreign policy."[22]

Truman's shipboard statement had not mentioned Vice President Nixon's turbulent visit to Latin America in May 1958, but on his return from France in July, he found an invitation from Senator Mike Monroney inviting him to attend the Interparliamentary Union meeting in Brazil later that summer. Replying to Monroney's invitation on 18 July, concerning the Interparlia-mentary meeting in Rio de Janeiro, Truman answered that he would be unable to attend. "All I want," he replied, "is to help keep the peace and try to restore the friendships we had with our neighbors in times past." Monroney, in fact, had hoped that Mr. Truman could attend the Rio meeting in order to offset "the bad experience" of Nixon's South American visit, as his letter attests. "My personal feelings," Monroney added, "are that you would be given an entirely different reception, because of the record you made in Latin America...and the love that these people know you have for them."[23]

Despite Truman's optimism, and his "hope that things will work out all right internationally," he remained as troubled by the Eisenhower-Nixon policies as home as he would remain troubled by U.S. policy over Berlin, and, soon after, over Cuba and Vietnam. Understandably, then, and for the next several years, problems in foreign relations left little incentive to travel, or so it seemed. Writing to Frank Conniff of the Hearst news organization in January 1960, Truman stated that there was little "possibility" of his "going abroad [that] year to Europe, Russia or the Far East, all of which I would like to do but conditions are such that I must stay at home."[24]

Previously, the Greek government had hoped to persuade the Trumans to visit Greece, but it was not until the installation of a Democratic president that an opportunity materialized. It was not long after, in fact, in May 1961, when Truman spoke by phone from the White House with the Greek Prime Minister, Constantine Karamanlis, that the invitation was made. The State Department also favored the idea, as Mr. Truman's visit "would further our objective of strengthening the ties between Greece and the United States," the State Department's Lucius Battle communicated to the White House on 16 May. Alas, however, Truman wrote to President Kennedy on 30 June 1961, declining the invitation thus extended by the Greek government through its ambassador in Washington, saying that he and Mrs. Truman were "not in a position...to do that, much as we would like to."[25] It was not until the death of King Paul in March 1964, that Truman could be persuaded to fly to Athens at the request of another president, accompanied by Mrs. Lyndon Johnson as the president's personal representative. While he had been moved by such a request, he must also have recalled the gratitude of the Greek nation the year before, when that nation unveiled a statue in his honor. As Truman had written Prime Minister Karamanlis of Greece on that occasion: "I have always had an idea that statues should not be erected to people until they have been dead ten years." He went on to say, however, that he was "highly pleased," because the Greek and Turkish aid program had been "one of the highlights" of those years, in 1947 and 1948.[26]

As it turned out, the following year was also the end of an era of goodwill diplomacy, since former President Truman was not again to make another trip abroad after 1964.

CHAPTER VIII: POST-MEMOIRS ACCOUNTS AND THE PEACE INSTITUTE

LATER WRITINGS

Following the publication of his *Memoirs* and two trips abroad between 1956 and 1958, Mr. Truman published two further accounts: *Mr. Citizen*, a record of his early post-White House years, and *Truman Speaks*, a series of talks he gave at Columbia University in April 1959. Both accounts were published in 1960, and both reflected a "hands-on" approach to public affairs which had characterized his years of presidential service. As Leon Keyserling, one of his former advisers, recalled: "despite his great knowledge of American history and the history of the Presidency, [he] always dealt in a pragmatic and factual manner with the issues before him."[1] In his post-memoirs account, *Mr. Citizen*, the title Mr. Truman chose to call his book in rendering an account of his post-presidential activities, the themes of public import discussed were not unlike those of his Radner lectures at Columbia University.

The themes dealt with education, the presidency and Constitution, and, not least, with the U.N. At Columbia, for example, he had shown the Bill of Rights to be an indispensable guide to understanding the "individual and his rights" in what he termed the "greatest part of the Constitution," that presidential responsibility for the general welfare is paramount—a perennial theme—because only the "President is the representative of the whole nation," and that free government is best served by an educated citizenry. Another recurrent theme concerned the importance he attached to American support of the U.N. as "the best hope of achieving a better world."[2]

As he said, in addressing the U.N. issue, "I don't know how long it will take," but if factionalism can be kept within bounds, "we'll make the United Nations...work, and we will then be settling things by international law instead of atomic bombs." He looked, then, to the U.N. Charter, as he looked to the nation's Constitution, in helping to safeguard "fundamental freedoms"; thus he had hoped for the eventual acceptance of an international

Bill of Rights, acceptable to the majority of the U.N. member states, as he had earlier recommended in testimony before the Senate in its review of the U.N. Charter in 1955. What he feared was that the world body would not adopt a Bill of Rights and that, as he cautioned the students and faculty at Columbia, if and when the U.N. "quits working," world peace would be threatened along with the threat of another world war. In short, he envisioned no alternative to the U.N. and U.N. agencies as a means of preserving peace and in providing, however imperfectly, a modicum of world order in the years to come. Perhaps the Dean of Columbia College best typified reaction to Truman's Radner talks in his letter to him of 17 May 1959: "Your three day visit at Columbia did more for the college students," Dean Palfrey wrote, "than any other occasion in my experience here."[3]

And in June 1960, when the former president addressed a much larger audience on the occasion of the fifteenth anniversary of the founding of the United Nations in San Francisco, he again, as he had at Columbia, stressed the importance of the U.N. in helping to improve worldwide living standards through economic and technical assistance that had become a part of the U.N.'s work. He also cited the importance of the U.N.'s role in thwarting armed aggression, even among those states "that may be strong enough to violate it."[4]

Another common theme between his Radner talks and *Mr. Citizen* had been Mr. Truman's reflections on the office and duties of the president. Indeed, Truman was probably the first modern president to elaborate on the president's six duties in a number of his speeches, as in *Truman Speaks*. And his frankness was especially focused on the president's central role as the key decision-maker in domestic and foreign affairs; that is, as the only official "elected by the whole people," and "responsible to the whole people." Again, it is also this duty more than any other that he dwells upon in *Mr. Citizen*: of the president as someone who knows that every fear and every hope of his fellow citizens "falls within the scope of his concern," and "that it is the President's responsibility to look at all questions from the point of view of the whole people." As such powers are not "explicitly" set out in Article II, they "are powers which no President can pass on to his successor," but "go only to the man who can take and use them." So stated, the wise use of these powers "can make a Jefferson or a Lincoln Administration," whereas "their non-use can make a Buchanan or a Grant Administration," he concluded.[5]

Truman's reasoning underscored yet another presidential duty not explicitly found in Article II: the president's leadership of his own party, as emphasized in *Mr. Citizen*. Hence his further conclusion that leadership of party and executive responsibility for the general welfare stand together, another "deciding" reason, as he put it, "for...remaining a Democrat," in contrast to the views of the Republican Party on the chief executive's responsibility for the general welfare. His reasoning is altogether apparent in the chapter entitled "Some Thoughts on the Presidency," as leadership of party and executive responsibility for the general welfare have not stood up under most Republican administrations, he maintained, because the Republican Party has remained "suspicious" of strong executive leadership.[6]

Likewise, though the president's other duties are explicitly enumerated in the Constitution, Mr. Truman preferred to view these as well—and properly so—in historical perspective. So too, the president's broad responsibility as commander in chief provides a case in point, as in his Radner lectures, as Truman's attitude toward military spending had been one of placing limits on Pentagon expenditures. Similarly, as he had reminded his audience at Columbia: "It's [the President's] privilege to appoint generals—and sometimes to fire them when it's necessary."[7]

Two further accounts, either dictated or recorded during these years, were never made public during Mr. Truman's lifetime. The earlier account, published the year after his death in 1973, had been based on taped interviews with Mr. Truman in the years 1961 and 1962. Entitled *Plain Speaking: An Oral Biography of Harry S. Truman*, it had been compiled by the writer and former World War II correspondent, Merle Miller, whereas the later account, *Where the Buck Stops: The Personal and Private*

Writings of Harry S. Truman, and edited by his daughter Margaret, was not published until 1989.

In *Plain Speaking*, the image of Mr. Truman's hands-on approach to public affairs remains undiminished, although it differs in language and content to some extent from the earlier volumes. *Mr. Citizen*, for example, which is almost bland by comparison to Miller's sometimes biting account, had been edited by two men frequently seen together in Independence, and friends of Mr. Truman, William Hillman and David Noyes. *Plain Speaking*, however, is feisty and humorous, and occasionally profane and low-down in expression. But it is also a serious book in the series of messages it conveys, even though questions continue to be raised about the book's lack of documentation, and hence its authenticity.[8] Adding to the heightened interest in its contents, as *Plain Speaking* had been a best-seller, was the fact that the taped interviews with Truman were never aired publicly, though that had been their intended purpose.

Nonetheless, the contents of the Truman-Miller interviews should confirm much of what is reported in *Plain Speaking*, once the taped interviews have been opened to research students, since the "Finding Aid" of the interviews reveal a former president discussing a whole range of issues, subjects, and personages which have become familiar to students of the Truman era: the 1948 campaign, McCarthyism, Point Four, on learning from history, the need for international law, the Korean conflict and U.N. participation, the future of the U.N., Adlai Stevenson, on Jefferson and Jackson versus the "special interests," on military men as politicians, on the five weak presidents before the Civil War, on his advice to young politicians, and on the presidents after the Civil War—Grant, Hayes, Garfield, Arthur, and Cleveland—among other topics.[9]

Truman, though, always seemed to come back to the subjects of the presidency and of learning from history. If, in fact, the latter is a guide to conduct, as he believed, he held equally firm to the idea that the president alone has the duty to act on behalf of the general welfare. "Everything," as he said, "belongs to the people. I was just privileged to *use* it for a while," he apparently told Miller in referring to the presidency. As he had said, this was an important reason for knowing about the nature of the presidency, since the office has been essential to understanding "the country and how we got it," as much as an understanding of the nation's history has and would be essential in guiding its citizenry in the future.[10] Truman thus identified "free government" with the president's responsibility under the Constitution to promote the general welfare. Free government, then, works only if those "in charge...have the welfare of the people in mind at all times..." It was also the reason, he acknowledged, why he "was never...happy about the fellow [who] succeeded me," in reference to his successor's failure to grasp the relationship between the presidency and the welfare of the people, and as evidenced at differing periods in the nation's past.[11]

And in *Where the Buck Stops*, Mr. Truman elaborates more fully on this same theme. In what is really "a handbook for Presidents," his general and immediate observation on the history of the presidency seems almost unforgettable: "that history is made in our country by men who have the welfare of the people in their minds," and who had "to make frequent and difficult decisions in order to get that done." He added that "there are about six or seven men who understood the presidency" in this sense, and "at least that many who paid no attention to their powers and duties; that is...they didn't exercise the powers that were given them under the Constitution..."[12]

Had not, in fact, Mr. Truman indicated in that remarkably frank statement on the presidency what kind of book ought to be written in order to validate his conclusions about the institution's historic link between the duties of the office and the general welfare, and the maintenance of free society?

Indeed, this was Jeffersonianism only a modern Jeffersonian could tell it: When the "favored few" control the national government "by controlling the finances of the country," not only the general welfare but free government are thereby threatened. In such circumstances, as Truman makes abundantly clear, the president is not performing his duties under the Constitution if special or "vested interests," public or private, are allowed to dominate presidential policy. Whether it is a Nicholas Biddle or an August Belmont, or an Allan Sproul, whom he termed "economic royalists," the question remained whether the "money problem" would be resolved in favor of the few at the top or the many at the bottom. Truman thus maintained that for anything beneficial for the general welfare to occur, the president must be able to make decisions to offset the financial and political power of "economic royalists," and that the chief executives who could not make such decisions were "the ones who caused all the trouble."[13]

As this viewpoint was a powerful indictment of such individuals and groups, so Truman was unswerving in his criticism of presidential policy that ignored this reality, whether in word or in deed. Quoting approvingly from Jefferson's letter to Henry Lee, Jefferson had made the same observation in his letter of 10 August 1824, if less dramatically. "Men...are naturally divided into two parties," Jefferson wrote: "Those who fear and distrust the people, and wish to draw all powers from them...[and] those who identify themselves with the people...as the most honest and safe...de-pository of the public interests."[14]

Alas, as Truman also points out in *Where the Buck Stops*, the problems associated with "economic royalists" are not limited to the domestic sphere, but extend to the nation's foreign affairs, as occurred in the area of foreign trade prior to the passage of the Reciprocal Trade Act of 1934. Again, as with the League of Nations and the Republican Party under Harding, the Republicans proved unwilling to favor a policy in the national interest, though they lacked an alternative policy of their own. By contrast, since Truman believed that the League of Nations would not have collapsed if the United States had been a member, so he believed "that World War II might have been avoided..." Consequently, he continued to worry about "special interests" in getting "control of a country," and of the "tremendous difficulties" that ensue.[15]

116

As much, therefore, as Truman looked to the success of free government at home, so he pinned his hopes on the eventual success of the U.N. in the international arena. As he had said on numerous occasions during his lifetime, so be belatedly conveyed in *Where the Buck Stops*: that as he had been "strong for the League of Nations," so he remained about its successor. He believed, he said, "that [the U.N.] will succeed if we just give it enough of a chance." Again, Mr. Truman had viewed the U.N. Charter as he viewed the Constitution in the earlier years of the Republic, as still "very young." And in the last chapter of *Where the Buck Stops*, he concluded: "I still feel that the United Nations will eventually bring about world peace..."[16]

HIS QUEST FOR PEACE

Assuredly, then, Truman's interest in the U.N. as humankind's best hope for a better world remained undiminished during the last years of his life. As he had written to one of the benefactors of the proposed building to be dedicated to the advancement of peace and erected in Jerusalem: "Any...program that is well calculated to advance man's hopes for a world living in peace will always engage my wholehearted support." After nearly a decade of relative quiet in the Middle East, the idea of lending his name to a proposed Peace Center in Jerusalem doubtless appealed to the former president, as did the idea that its purposes would be conducive to promoting "peace research" and, to the extent possible, such practical measures as soil conservation, flood control, and desalinization of sea water.[17]

In thus agreeing to lend his name to such a Peace Center it remained an open question whether the theoretical and practical aims of peace could be realized in an academic setting, since the proposed center would be affiliated with the Hebrew University of Jerusalem. In the 1950s, for example, when the Rockefeller Foundation sought to fund such a project, it had been contemplated that Arab and Jewish scholars might be willing to establish a joint Institute of Semitic Studies in Jerusalem, and that such an institute would have the backing of the Israeli government. Yet the proposed project got nowhere, according to the Rockefeller Foundation, because the Arabs refused to entertain such a "cooperative educational institute in the Middle East."[18]

In contrast to the approach of the Rockefeller Foundation, the initiative taken to erect a new building on the campus of the Hebrew University in Jerusalem had been the "brainchild" of Jewish leaders and admirers of the former president some ten years later when Mr. Truman was asked to lend his name to the project and its purposes on 15 October 1965. Altogether there were thirty-eight founders and three sponsors who had pledged their support, each agreeing to contribute $100,000 toward the establishment there of such a Peace Center.[19]

Inaugurated at the Truman Library in Independence on 20 January 1966, Eliahu Elath, then president of the Hebrew University, spoke of the historic decision made by President Truman eighteen years before, on 14 May 1948, when he extended *de facto* recognition only eleven minutes after the proclamation by Israel of its independence. In recalling that historic moment, Elath said, his university wished to express its gratitude by naming the building "the Harry S. Truman Center for the Advancement of Peace." Elath went on to say that the center would conduct "studies and research in subjects relating to international relations…as international law…comparative religion, political theory and philosophy, with emphasis on problems in education." He also spoke of plans to develop special projects conducive to Israel's experience in social and cultural integration of plural communities," as well as in related work "with the newly emergent and developing nations in Asia and Africa."[20]

The inaugural, which included President Johnson, Chief Justice Earl Warren, and thirty-six of the original founders of the center, included representatives from other countries, as Canada, the Philippines, and Israel, along with members of both Houses of Congress. Above all, the inaugural seemed to provide a "fresh start" for peace, as Truman's subsequent address, delivered by David Noyes in Jerusalem that July, likewise conveyed. The event had even prompted Senator Edward V. Long of Missouri to nominate the former president for "the 1966 Nobel Peace Prize" when he wrote the Norwegian Nobel Institute soon after; and, in due course, when Truman learned of this, thanked him for his "thoughtfulness."[21]

Mr. Truman, of course, had wanted to attend the groundbreaking ceremony for the Truman Center in July, but his physician and family dissuaded him from doing so. In consequence, a month after his eighty-second birthday, he asked that Vice President Hubert Humphrey be designated to represent him in Jerusalem, as he indicated by letter to Humphrey on 9 June: "You were my first and only choice to represent me for this eventful occasion," adding that he looked forward to their meeting again when he returned from Jerusalem. In an odd display of presidential decision-making, however, Johnson refused Truman's request. In his place, Truman obtained the acceptance of Thurgood Marshall, the solicitor general, who accompanied David Noyes, and Truman's personal secretary, Rose Conway, "as an indication of his personal interest."[22]

The choice of Thurgood Marshall to represent Mr. Truman on the occasion of the dedication there on 11 July had been, nevertheless, a blessing in disguise. Marshall, who had "been associated with the struggle for civil rights," received prolonged applause when he rose to speak before some 600 people gathered there for the ceremony in the university auditorium. The occasion, he remarked, was unprecedented. "In a smoldering world, we here give physical embodiment to our...capacity of reason and science to bank the fires of violence, to seek out the causes of war, to layout the paths to peace,"[23] he exclaimed.

Earlier, in keeping with his long-held interest in seeing Arabs and Jews "agree to the internationalization of Jerusalem," the former president expressed the hope that he would live to see the sinews of peace there "significantly advanced" before he passed on. Similarly, the mayor of Jerusalem, Teddy Kollek, hoped that some day the Peace Center would "serve both sides of the city," inasmuch as Jerusalem had been divided since 1948. Noyes, too, whom Mr. Truman had designated as his spokesman for the Peace Center, hoped that Jordan might be persuaded to grant extraterritorial rights for the building to be constructed on Mount Scopus, the highest hill overlooking the city, as Mount Scopus incorporated the Jordanian sector of Jerusalem. In fact, less than a week before the center's dedication, a group of students urged that the old campus on Mount Scopus, then a demilitarized enclave, be reopened as a peace university devoted to Middle Eastern studies, and be opened to both Arabs and Jews.[24]

The intervening months, between July 1966 and June 1967, came to belie these hopes, however. Instead of "constructive advances in the realm of man's relationship to man," the project soon became "mired in academic and procedural matters," and without any effective or apparent direction. Overshadowing these academic disputes, moreover, had been the mounting military aid being provided the Egyptians by the Soviet Union and the expected gains that would result in any conflict with Israel, since Egypt could also expect the support of Syria and Jordan.[25]

Soviet arms had thus come to fuel a long and resistant crisis in Arab-Israeli relations, as illustrated by the fact that overall Soviet aid to Egypt between 1954 and 1967 accounted for more than forty percent of Moscow's Third World aid. Further, in the spring of 1967 several Arab states took steps that increased the military threat to Israel, including the organizing of a joint Arab command and a stepped up war of words against Israel. In consequence, the threat of a third Arab-Israeli war in fact erupted on 5 June 1967, when Israel preempted. As Truman wrote to one of the center's key founders on the eve of Israel's attack: "The situation has again turned grim in that part of the world—and I hope it is contained before it gets out of hand."[26]

Grim, indeed, had been the outbreak of war from the standpoint of U.S. policy in the region, and after its outbreak in trying to keep Jordan neutral. The war had also been a grim reminder of the malevolence of Soviet policy, as Moscow proceeded to break diplomatic relations with Israel and rearm the defeated Arab armies in the aftermath of the "Six Day War." The war had also been a setback for the Peace Center and for any "practical measures" for peace, as contemplated in 1965 and 1966, as the center's directors pulled back from any commitments along these lines. It was an untoward turn of events, especially for Noyes in representing Mr. Truman's interest in the project. While the decision to remove the site to Mount Scopus no longer entailed the question of extraterritorial rights, since Jordan lost its half of the city and the West Bank in not remaining neutral, the center's rededication on 27 March 1968, nearly two years later, prompted an even stronger statement on Truman's behalf than in 1966; namely, that the center should concern itself less with the academic study "of war and peace" issues and more with "problems that affect the lives of the masses of people," as in the "areas of food, health, shelter," and irrigation. Similarly, Truman's statement again reasserted the overall importance of the U.N.'s mission in these areas, and that the Peace Center "will always stand ready to help when called upon."[27]

Thus began what was later referred to as the "war within the peace institute": between Noyes, as Mr. Truman's spokesman, in wanting the center to adopt an active agenda in working for peace and so in not wanting the center to be "overcommitted to academic disciplines," and the center's directors in wanting to refrain from any activist role in favor of research on Third World problems, including the Middle East. Noyes had even suggested the building of a radio station, and changing the center's name to give it a wider identity, to be called "The Truman International Center for the Advancement of Peace."[28]

Nevertheless, the idea of reviving some aspects of Mr. Truman's original Point Four program appealed to the center's directors on humanitarian and related grounds, and under the heading of "special projects" there seemed to be a meeting of minds. But on the substantive issue of engaging in other practical pursuits, Noyes had not been able to make much headway. In the end, Mr. Truman, who was seldom to be seen "going and coming" from his office at the library in Independence, even before the Peace Center's rededication in March 1967, was less than enthusiastic three years later about the center's restrictive mission in opting to limit "its activities to research."[29] Its name was also modified, however slightly, to reflect its more limited purpose to "The Harry S. Truman Research Institute for the Advancement of Peace."

CHAPTER IX: THE POST-WHITE HOUSE YEARS IN PERSPECTIVE

TRUMAN AND HIS LEGACY

Truman's post-White House years started out, as noted in the first chapter, with the former president and his wife returning to Independence "empty handed." Nevertheless, it was Mr. Truman's refusal to lend his name and the office he had held to any kind of commercial venture for profit which set him apart, out of deference to that position, as an example of selfless public service to the nation.

The Congress, of which he had been a member, had passed a pension act for its members in 1942, only to be repealed because of public opposition against "congressional avarice" in wartime. When Congress passed a new pension act after World War II, it did not include ex-presidents. Thus, until August 1958, Mr. Truman's only pension had been his retirement pay of less than $120 dollars a month as a colonel in the Army reserves.[1] Again, since he received no federal pension—nor had any president before him—he had also been without any Secret Service protection since leaving Washington in January 1953.

Eventually, to relieve Mr. Truman's "financial plight," Congress passed the Former Presidents Act in 1958, and thereby established the office of ex-president. As Herbert Hoover, the only other ex-president, told newsmen at the time, he was in favor of the bill before Congress to award a $25,000 yearly pension. "It could be used either to support the families of former Presidents or it could be used for charity," adding that "former Presidents have had to take on a lot of public duties. They are semi-public servants."[2]

In recommending federal funding for retired presidents, along with a $10,000 annual pension for their widows, the bill had included a $50,000 annual sum for maintaining an office and staff, and free mailing privileges. "We expect a former President to engage in no business or occupation which would demean the office...or capitalize upon it in any improper way," the Senate held in its deliberations in supporting passage of the Former

Presidents Act. Writing from France on 1 July 1958, on the eve of his return by ship to New York, Mr. Truman expressed relief about the "committee report" favoring its passage, as he wrote to "Charlie" Murphy, adding that it "is good news, not for me personally but for all the people who are working for me in the office at Independence. They can now look forward to a future if this bill passes."[3]

Good news also came belatedly in 1963, in the form of a Senate Resolution, that permitted former presidents to use the Senate "as a forum whenever they wished." The Senate's action in this matter had pleased Truman, as he, in fact, "became the first ex-President to address the Senate in formal session" the following year on the occasion of his eightieth birthday. "I had spoken to the Senate once before," he recalled, in April 1960, but on that occasion the Senate "had to go through the formality of taking a recess."[4]

That year, as it turned out, also marked a turning point in Mr. Truman's involvement in public affairs during his post-White House years. It had, for example, marked the last time he would serve his country as a goodwill ambassador; it also marked the occasion of his last commencement address, when he spoke to the graduating class at Westminister College in Fulton, Missouri, on 8 June 1964. It was there also that he again spoke about the presidency, and about presidential papers, suggesting that "all the personal utterances of U.S. presidents be recorded in a cumulative publication,...boresome or not." As Westminister's president, Robert L.D. Davidson, wrote the former president a few days later: "Your inimitable quality of forthrightness and conviction has once more stirred our hearts and...to be grateful for your talents in so many areas of human relations."[5]

What had continued to enliven and ennoble Truman's speeches until 1964 had been his preoccupation with the unique importance of the presidency in the public life of the nation. That preoccupation, in fact, had been equalled only by his veneration of the office and his interest in those who had occupied it before him. Fortunately, that same preoccupation also imbued his outlook and thought on education, the realm he viewed as the ultimate basis of the nation's security. And so, as "education for responsibility" shaped his views about education's relation to the sustenance of free society, so education for responsibility had shaped his outlook about education's role in the maintenance of free government.[6] Indeed, such preoccupations explain much about Mr. Truman's outlook and probity as an ex-president, about his near obsession with his party's fortunes, as a "semi-public" servant and correspondent, and as the legatee of the position he had held and revered.

In 1964, for example, this same emphasis on the unique importance of the presidency in public life explained why he refused a TV network's offer of $50,000 "to be a commentator" at that year's Democratic National Convention. He had rejected the offer for the same reason he had "turned down" such offers more than a decade earlier—as he had said on that occasion: "Of course, they didn't want me, they wanted the Presidency." Ironically, when former President Eisenhower was offered the same amount by the American Broadcasting Company to be "an analyst" at the 1964 Republican National Convention, he accepted. As James Clark, the author of *Faded Glory: Presidents Out of Power*, noted, it was "the only starring role he was to play," despite the fact that Eisenhower's "influence over the convention was nil."[7]

Indeed, it is in Truman's outlook, then, where one finds another ex-president who stands alongside the "six or seven" others who understood and acted upon the president's prerogatives in looking after the general welfare; it is in Truman's outlook where one finds an ex-president who understood the importance of the Bill of Rights and of "due process" in protecting the liberties of the American people, even though there remain some who thought that he should have done more. It is in Truman's outlook where one finds another Bill of Rights being advocated; one he hoped that the member states of the United Nations would agree upon in time.[8] And it is in Truman's outlook where one finds a former president more concerned about what others think of his country than of his own place in history.

As he often said in his post-White House speeches, the president has "six jobs" to perform; and if, under modern conditions, the chief executive is not performing all six, the president is not carrying out the duties of the office in accordance with the president's responsibility in representing the people at large. As he well noted in talks with students on the subject of the presidency: "the President has the ultimate responsibility for the conduct of the entire executive branch of the government", and "is the only elected official...alone...responsible to the people."[9]

All told, this was surely Truman's legacy to his countrymen.

APOTHEOSIS

The searchlight of Truman's thought on the presidency thus remains as his ultimate legacy to the nation, as instanced by the importance he assigned to the link between the presidency and the general welfare. The heart of the problem of American society, as he knew, concerned the dangers to democratic government which came from the same people who called themselves liberal, though, in his view, could hardly be called "democratic." Their liberalism—irrespective of party labels—had been little more than a mask for unbridled "individualism" and unbridled capitalism with little or no concern for the general welfare. Again, as the former president warned, this problem had to be met head-on, and met head-on by the president, if the "special interests," masked in the name of liberalism, were not to threaten and overwhelm free society and the general welfare.[10] Consequently, Truman had an intense interest in preserving presidential papers, in establishing the *Public Papers of the Presidents* project in 1957, and in completing the Truman Library in Independence that same year in order to aid and guide future generations.[11]

As noted in the preceding pages, it is apparent that Truman looked upon the general welfare as the key to understanding American democracy. The point seems almost elementary. With the lapse of a commitment to the general welfare on the part of the chief executive, free government and democracy are thereby weakened, whereas a commitment to democratic ends promotes the general welfare and free society. So too, he believed, the president must work for peace through the United Nations and for a better world through U.S. support of international law. It might even be said that without Truman's unfailing support of the U.N. between 1945 and 1953, the dangers to world peace and the U.N.'s future may have been greater than they had been during those same years of trial and hope.

Mr. Truman, lastly, never held an imperial vision of America's future, despite the far-flung policies that he had pursued as president to defend the Free World. As Britain's prime minister had told him as he was about to leave office in January

1953: "I misjudged you badly," Churchill told Truman. "Since [1945]…, you, more than any other man, have saved Western civilization."[12] Nor had Truman pursued policies that he thought might be harmful to the average citizen in defense of the status quo. On the contrary, like Jefferson, he had trusted and believed in the average citizen as the best means of preserving "free government"; and he stood opposed to those who would weaken the president's conduct of foreign policy by constitutional amendment and, at the other extreme, by those who might or would involve the nation in ruinous war. Not, in fact, since Woodrow Wilson had the nation been represented by a president who had been more "sensitive to the constitutional origins of the Presidency."[13]

In saying all of this, the purpose has not been to venerate Mr. Truman but to point out how he had tried to relate the experience of those years, 1945 to 1953, to the unfinished tasks that he had set for himself during the years of his retirement: years in which he had sought to render some contribution to the continuing quest for democracy and peace until he could no longer do so for reasons of health.

Indeed, when Truman passed away on December 26, 1972, it had already seemed apparent that the former president had been "one of America's greatest presidents," as Richard Kirkendall stated in a memorial address on 17 January 1973. And in paying tribute to Mr. Truman *apropos* of his foreign policy as president, Kirkendall noted: "Truman believed that the United States could and should play a large role in world affairs," but that the United States could not "do all that it might wish nor accomplish all that it might hope."[14] In short, Truman's vision of America's world role was not limitless, because it was rooted in an understanding of America's past and in history's lessons—for good or ill.

In conclusion, it remains to be seen whether Truman's democratic vision of America, and of its non-imperial world role, will be heeded in the years to come.

NOTES:

INTRODUCTION

1.   Joseph P. Baratta, "Internationalism," *The Harry S. Truman Encyclopedia*: Edited by Richard S. Kirkendall (Boston: G.K. Hall & Co., 1989), p. 175.

2.   Harry S. Truman, "The Future for Young Americans," *St. Louis Post-Dispatch*, Sunday Supplement, December 13, 1953, p. 5.

3.   Truman, "The Future for Young Americans," p. 5.

4.   Margaret Truman, *Harry S. Truman* (New York: William Morrow & Co., 1973), p. 401: Arthur F. McClure and Donna Costigan, "The Truman Vice Presidency: Constructive Apprenticeship or Brief Interlude?", *Missouri Historical Review*, Vol. LXV, No. 3 (April, 1971), pp. 340-41.

5.   Margaret Truman (ed.), *Where the Buck Stops: The Personal and Private Writings of Harry S. Truman* (New York: Warner Books, 1989), p. 203. Hereinafter cited as *Where the Buck Stops*.

6.   Martin Gilbert, *Winston S. Churchill, Vol. VIII: 'Never Despair,' 1945-1965* (Boston: Houghton Mifflin Co., 1988), p. 676.

7.   U.S. Congress, Senate, *Hearings Before a Subcommittee of the Committee on Foreign Relations; Proposal to Amend or Otherwide Modify Existing Peace and Security Organizations, Including the U.N., Part 12*, 84th Cong., 1st Sess., Truman's testimony, April 18, 1955 (Washington: U.S. Government Printing Office, 1955), p. 1619. Hereinafter cited as *U.N. Hearings*.

8.   Harry S. Truman, *Truman Speaks* (New York: Columbia University Press, 1960), p. 114.

9.   George E. Reedy, *The Twilight of the Presidency: From Johnson to Reagan*, Rev. ed. (New York: New American Library, 1970, 1987), p. 179.

10.   Truman to Richard L. Neuberger, February 13, 1956, Harry S. Truman Papers, Post-Presidential Files (Name File), Box 64, Truman Library.   Hereinafter cited as Truman Papers, PPF.

CHAPTER 1: THE TRANSITION, 1953

1. Wilson Brown, "Aide to Four Presidents," *American Heritage*, Vol. 4, No. 2 (February 1955), p. 96.
2. "Text of Truman's Farewell as President," *New York Times*, January 16, 1953, p. 12.
3. "Truman's Farewell," *New York Times*, p. 12.
4. "Truman's Farewell," *New York Times*, p. 12.
5 Omar N. Bradley to Truman, January 21, 1953; Truman Papers, PPF (Name File), Box 12.
6. Louis B. Wright, "Harry S. Truman: A Defender of Learning," *Congressional Record—Appendix*, 84th Cong., 1st Sess., June 20, 1955, p. A4462.
7. Robert H. Ferrell (ed.), *Off the Record: The Private Papers of Harry S. Truman* (New York: Harper & Row, 1980), p. 288.
8. Truman's speech, Independence, February 5, 1953; Truman Papers, PPF (Speech File), Box 12. The turnout of some 10,000 people in Independence "surprised" Mr. Truman and his wife; Francis H. Heller, "After the Presidency: The Case of Harry S. Truman" (Unpublished MS, n.d.), pp. 3-4.
9. Harry S. Truman, *Mr. Citizen* (New York: Bernard Geis Associates, 1960), pp. 57-58.
10. Roy Jenkins, *Truman* (New York: Harper & Row, 1986), p. 209.
11. John Whiteclay Chambers, II, "Presidents Emeritus," *American Heritage* (June/July 1979), Vol. 30, No. 4, p. 24; James Giglio, "Harry S. Truman and the Multifarious Ex-Presidency," *Presidential Studies Quarterly*, Vol. XII, No. 2 (Spring 1982), p. 248.
12. "Truman on TV: Sets Aims for Youth," *New York Times*, September 21, 1953, p. 13.
13. Truman to John A. Burns, February 26, 1953; Truman Papers, PPF (Trip File), Box 1.
14. Truman to Arthur W. Radford, February 26, 1953; Truman Papers, PPF (Trip File), Box 1; Truman to Gregg M. Sinclair, April 11, 1953; Truman Papers, PPF (Trip File), Box 1.

15. Memo, Truman to Admiral Radford, April 4, 1953; Truman Papers, PPF (Trip File), Box 1. See also, *Off the Record*, pp. 290-91.

16. Speech (draft), Truman's address, University of Hawaii, April 24, 1953; Truman Papers, PPF (Trip File), Box 1.

17. Truman to Charles MacLeod, April 14, 1953; Truman Papers, PPF (Trip File), Box 1.

18. Truman to Mrs. Robert P. Patterson, April 24, 1953; Truman Papers, PPF (Trip File), Box 1.

19. Speech, May 12, 1953; see *New York Times*, May 13, 1953, pp. 1, 8.

20. Truman to Clark M. Clifford, February 7, 1953; Truman Papers, PPF (Secretary's Office File), Box 28; *New York Times*, February 22, 1953, p.1.

21. *New York Times*, February 22, 1953; p. 44.

22. Truman to George M. Elsey, February 23, 1954; Truman Papers, PPF (Name File), Box 26. See also, *Mr. Citizen*, pp. 55-56.

23. David D. Lloyd to Truman, July 31, 1953 (Memoir Folder), Papers of David D. Lloyd, Truman Library, Box 14. See also, Dave Bell to Lloyd, July 12, 1953; Papers of Charles S. Murphy, Truman Library, Box 17. Hereinafter cited as the Lloyd Papers and Murphy Papers.

24. Truman to Kenneth W. Hechler, August 5, 1953; Truman Papers, PPF (General File), Box 7.

25. Meeting of the Board of Trustees, Kansas City, Missouri, March 5, 1953; Truman Papers (Harry S. Truman Library, Inc.), Box 24.

26. Annual Meeting of the Board of Trustees, September 19, 1953; Truman Papers (Harry S. Truman Library, Inc.), Box 46.

27. Truman to Dean Acheson, October 2, 1953; Truman Papers, PPF (Trip File), Box 2. Nonetheless, only the Rockefeller Foundation responded positively.

28. Truman to Acheson, April 24, 1953; Truman Papers, PPF (Name File), Box 1.

29. W. Averell Harriman to Truman, May 15, 1953: Truman

Papers, PPF (Name File, Box 36; also, Harriman to Truman, June 2, 1953; Truman Papers, PPF (Name File), Box 36.

30. Memorandum, "Thoughts on the HST speech at Detroit," July 31, 1953; Truman Papers, PPF (Trip File), Box 2.

31. Speech, Truman's Labor Day address, September 7, 1953; Truman Papers, PPF (Trip File), Box 2.

32. Truman to Melvin D. Hildreth, September 27, 1954; Truman Papers, PPF (Name File), Box 62.

CHAPTER 2: AUTHOR AND LECTURER

1. Truman to Acheson, August 18, 1953; Truman Papers, PPF (Name File), Box 1; Truman to Stephen A. Mitchell, July 31, 1953; Truman Papers, PPF (Political File), Box 1.

2. Speech by W. Averell Harriman, Waldorf-Astoria, New York, September 28, 1953; Truman Papers, PPF (Trip File), Box 2.

3. Speech by former President Truman, New York City, February 5, 1954; Murphy Papers (Speech File), Box 17.

4. Truman, *Mr. Citizen*, p. 113.

5. "What Hysteria Does to Us," Harry S. Truman, *Freedom and Equality: Addresses* by Harry S. Truman, edited by David S. Horton (Columbia: University of Missouri Press, 1960), p. 65; *New York Times*, April 13, 1954.

6. *Daily Sun-Gazette*, Fulton, April 13, 1954, pp. 1-2; *The Columns* (Westminister College), April, 28, 1954, p.1.

7. "What Hysteria Does to Us," *Freedom and Equality*, p. 74.

8. Notes, (Green Lecture), n.d.; Truman Papers, PPF (Trip File), November 1953-May 1954, Box 3.

9. Francis H. Heller, "The Writing of the Truman Memoirs," *Presidential Studies Quarterly*, XIII, No. 1 (Winter 1983), pp. 81-83. Hillman and Noyes had indeed worked as a team in editing the memoirs, though, as Webster Schott suggests, Hillman's influence was probably greater. Webster Schott, "How the Memoirs Were Written," *The New Republic*, March 19, 1956, pp. 18-19.

10. Heller, "After the Presidency: The Case of Harry S. Truman" (MS, n.d.), pp. 8-10.

11. Heller, "After the Presidency: The Case of Harry S. Truman," p. 10.

12. Francis H. Heller, "The Memoirs of Harry S. Truman"; Remarks before the Jackson County Historical Society, May 18, 1958. (Copy provided by the JCHS, Archives & Research Library, Independence, Missouri); Heller, "After the Presidency: The Case of Harry S. Truman," p. 10.

13. Heller, "The Memoirs of Harry S. Truman"; Remarks before the Jackson County Historical Society, May 18, 1958.

14. Heller, "The Memoirs of Harry S. Truman"; Remarks before the Jackson County Historical Society, May 18, 1958.

15. Harry S. Truman, "Foreign Policy and National Defense," September 9, 1955, *Vital Speeches of the Day*, Vol. XXII, No. 1, October 15, 1955, p. 15.

16. Dean Acheson to President Truman, July 25, 1955; Truman Papers, PPF (Name File), Memoir Folder, Box 1; Jim F. Heath, *Decade of Disillusionment: The Kennedy-Johnson Years* (Bloomington: Indiana University Press, 1975), p. 6.

17. Matthew B. Ridgway, *The Korean War* (New York: Doubleday & Co., 1967), p. 148; Ferrell, *Off the Record*, pp. 303-04.

18. Dean Acheson to President Truman, June 25, 1955; Truman Papers, PPF (Name File), Memoir Folder, Box 1. The greater portion of this letter is reprinted in the collection of letters, *Among Friends: Personal Letters of Dean Acheson*, edited by David S. McLellan and D.C. Acheson (New York: Dodd, Mead and Co., 1980), pp. 99-107.

19. Dean Acheson to Truman, March 14, 1955; Truman Papers, PPF (Trip File), Box 4; Ridgway, *Korean War*, pp. 144-45, 155-56. Cf. Douglas MacArthur, *Reminiscences* (New York: McGraw-Hill Book Co., 1964), p. 378.

20. Francis Heller, "Truman," *The History Makers*, edited by Lord Longford and Sir John Wheeler-Bennett (New York: St. Martin's Press, 1973), p. 325.

21. Arthur H. Compton to Truman, April 26, 1955; Truman Papers, PPF (Name File), Box 19.

22. Arthur H. Compton, *Atomic Quest: A Personal Narrative* (New York: Oxford University Press, 1956), pp. 248-49.

23. Arthur H. Compton to Truman, August 27, 1955; Truman Papers, PPF (Name File), Box 19; Letter (Unsent), Truman to Herbert Feis, n.d.; Truman Papers, PPF (Secretary's Office File), Box 19.

24. Harry S. Truman, Memoirs: *Year of Decisions, Vol. I* (New York: Doubleday and Co., 1955), pp. 419-26.

25. W.J. Holmes to the author, October 16, 1981. Holmes, a former naval intelligence officer in Hawaii, wrote of his significant wartime experiences in *Double-Edged Secrets: U.S. Naval Intelligence Operations in the Pacific during World War II* (Annapolis: Naval Institute Press, 1979). See also, Forrest C. Pogue, *George C. Marshall: Statesman, 1945-1959* (New York: Viking, 1987), p. 23.

26. Harry S. Truman, *Memoirs, Years of Trial and Hope, Vol. II* (New York: Doubleday and Co., 1956), p. 106.

27. Thomas A. Bailey, *The American Pageant Revisited: Recollections of a Stanford Historian* (Stanford: Hoover Institution Press, 1982), p. 170.

28. William Hillman, *Mr. President* (New York: Farrar, Straus & Young, 1952), p. 249; Joseph M. Jones to Clark Clifford, November 23, 1949; Truman Papers (George M. Elsey Files), Box 41.

29. Howard Trivers, *Three Crises in American Foreign Policy and a Continuing Revolution* (Carbondale: Southern Illinois University Press, 1972), p. 100. See also, "The Sources of Soviet Conduct," *Foreign Affairs*, Vol. 25, No. 4 (July 1947), pp. 575-76.

30. "Sources of Soviet Conduct," *Foreign Affairs*, p. 582; George F. Kennan, *American Diplomacy, 1900-1950* (Chicago: University of Chicago Press, 1950), pp. 126-27.

31. Truman to Douglass Cater, July 31, 1956; (A copy of this letter was brought to the attention of the author by Douglass Cater.)

32. Truman, *Memoirs, I*, p.12. For reference to Lincoln's

democratic views and their dissipation by the Republican Party, see Walter Prescott Webb, "How the Republican Party Lost Its Future," *Southwest Review* (Autumn, 1949), pp. 329-36.

33. Truman, *Memoirs, I*, pp. 329-30.

34. Speech, Address by former President Truman in Saint Louis, February 2, 1957; Truman Papers (Secretary's Office File), Box 26.

35. Sir Oliver Franks, "Mr. Truman as President," *The Listener*, June 14, 1956, p. 788. See Also, Heller, "Truman," *The History Makers*, p. 335.

36. Eugene J. McCarthy, *The Hard Years: A Look at Contemporary America and American Institutions* (New York: The Viking Press, 1975), pp. 11, 98.

37. Eugene J. McCarthy, *Up 'Til Now; A Memoir* (San Diego: Harcourt Brace Jovanovich, Publishers, 1987), p. 10.

38. McCarthy, *Up 'Til Now*, p. 114; McCarthy, *The Hard Years*, pp. 4, 10.

39. Truman, *Memoirs, I*, p. 119.

40. Harry S. Truman. "My View of the Presidency," p. 1; Truman Papers, (General File), 1958, Box 1. For a brief discussion of the president's essential duties, see *Truman Speaks*, pp. 5-8.

41. Truman, "My View of the Presidency," p. 2.

42. Truman to Senator Estes Kefauver, June 16, 1961; Truman to Francis B. Burch, July 15, 1963; Truman Papers, PPF (Secretary's Office File).

43. Truman, *Mr. Citizen*, p. 225.

44. *Truman Speaks*, pp. 39-40; Reading copy of talk at Yale; Truman Papers, PPF (Trip File), 1958, Box 16.

45. *Where the Buck Stops*, pp. 342-43, 347-48; on education's link to the general welfare, see also, William T. Couch, *The Human Potential: An Essay On Its Cultivation* (Durham: Duke University Press, 1974), pp. 277-78, 366-67.

46. Truman, *Mr. Citizen*, p. 26. Robert Maynard Hutchins had been equally firm in linking the idea of freedom with liberal education. See his commentary on President Truman's Commission on Higher Education, "Report of the President's Commis-

sion on Higher Education," *Educational Record*, XXIX (April, 1948), pp. 107-22, and his earlier comments in *Education for Freedom* (Baton Rouge: Louisiana State University Press, 1943), pp. 14-17. Like the Presidency project, however, Mr. Truman's proposed history text never went beyond his instructive and imaginative outline for it; see the Outline, "What Every Boy and Girl Should Know About American History," n.d.; Truman Papers, PPF (Secretary's Office File), Box 10.

CHAPTER 3: BUILDING THE TRUMAN LIBRARY

1.   "Background Fact Sheet on the Harry S. Truman Library"; Harry S. Truman Library, Inc. (Dedication Folder), Box 5. Hereinafter cited as Truman Library, Inc. The early support of labor organizations was much in evidence, as the combined contributions of the Congress of Industrial Organizations, the CIO, and the United Steelworkers Union totalled $250,000. See the letter of David Lloyd to Basil O'Connor, December 23, 1954; Truman Papers, PPF (Name File), Box 52.

2.   Donald R. McCoy, *The National Archives: America's Ministry of Documents 1934-1968* (Chapel Hill: The University of North Carolina Press, 1978), p. 291.

3.   Margaret Truman, *Harry S. Truman*, p. 562.

4.   "Memorandum for the File," George M. Elsey, August 2, 1950, and K.W. Hechler's, "Memorandum for Mr. Elsey," August 3, 1950; Papers of George M. Elsey (Subject File), Box 98.

5.   "Memorandum for the President," David D. Lloyd, February 23, 1952; Truman Library, Inc. (Folder 1), 1951-54, Box 1; "The Truman Library," n.d.; Truman Library, Inc. (Records of the Treasurer), Box 54.

6.   "Background Fact Sheet on the Harry S. Truman Library," Truman Library, Inc.

7.   "Memorandum for the President," Advisory Committee for the Truman Library, David D. Lloyd, February 8, 1952; Papers of George M. Elsey (Subject File), Box 98.

8.   Memorandum, President Truman to David Lloyd, June 18, 1953 (Advisory Committee Folder); Truman Library, Inc.,

Box 31. As indicated at the beginning of this chapter, there were some historians who deplored the decentralization of presidential papers, even though there were probably few archivists, if any, who did not favor it.

9. David D. Lloyd, "The Harry S. Truman Library," *American Archivist*, Vol. 18, No. 2 (April 1955), p. 100; "Memorandum for the Record," Conversation with Wayne Grover on Truman Library, February 12, 1952; Truman Library, Inc. (Advisory Committee Folder), Box 31; "Memorandum for the President," Advisory Committee for Truman Library, David D. Lloyd, February 8, 1952, Attachment A, Panel of Suggestions for Advisory Committee; George M. Elsey Papers, Box 98.

10. Lloyd, "The Harry S. Truman Library," *The American Archivist* (1955), p. 107.

11. McCoy, *The National Archives*, p. 297.

12. U.S. Congress, House of Representatives, *Hearing Before a Special Subcommittee of the Committee on Government Operations* (Bill to Provide for the Acceptance and Maintenance of Presidential Libraries and for Other Purposes), 84th Cong., 1st Sess., June 13, 1955 (1955), p. 30.

13. House of Representatives, *Hearing Before a Special Subcommittee on Government Operations*, pp. 30, 56.

14. House of Representatives, *Hearing Before a Special Subcommittee on Government Operations*, "Statement of Henry Steele Commager...on Proposed Presidential Library Legislation," p. 61.

15. Copy, GSA News Release, August 12, 1955; Truman Library, Inc. (Officers and Trustees File Folder), Box 31.

16. David D. Lloyd to President Truman, February 8, 1955; Truman Papers, PPF (Name File), Box 52.

17. Philip C. Brooks, "The Harry S. Truman Library—Plans and Reality," *The American Archivist*, Vol. 25, No. 1 (January 1962), p. 31.

18. Address at Rollins College, March 8, 1949; *Harry S. Truman, Public Papers of the Presidents of the United States, 1949* (Wash.: Government Printing Office, 1964), p. 167.

19. Draft, "A Proposal for the Creation of a Harry S. Truman Library Institute," February 8, 1955; Truman Papers, PPF (Name File), Box 52.

20. Philip D. Lagerquist, "The Truman Library Institute: The First Years," *Whistle Stop* (Library Institute Newsletter), Vol. 14, No. 2, 1966; Minutes of Meeting of the Building Committee, Board of Trustees of the Harry S. Truman Library, April 16, 1955; Truman Library, Inc., Box 1.

21. David D. Lloyd to Edward F. Neild, February 10, 1954; Truman Library, Inc. (Architect folder, 1951-54), Box 1. While still in the White House, President Truman had called upon the firm of Neild and Somdal of Shreveport to draw up the basic design for his presidential library. Edward F. Neild had had long experience in the design of public buildings, and had been an architectural adviser at the time in the renovation of the White House.

22. R.P. Weatherford, Jr. to President Truman, June 14, 1954; Truman Papers, PPF (Name File), Box 90.

23. David Demarest Lloyd, "Presidential Papers and How They Grew," *The Reporter*, February 2, 1954, pp. 31-34. On Truman's speeches on the presidency and on the importance of presidential papers, see, e.g., his speech in New York on 8 May 1954; *New York Times*, May 9, 1954, p. 54.

24. David D. Lloyd to Edwin W. Pauley, May 27, 1954; Truman Library, Inc., Box 34.

25. David D. Lloyd to President Truman, August 27, 1954; Lloyd Papers (Truman File Folder, 1954-59), Truman Library, Box 13. At the time, only Executive Orders and Messages to Congress were published, respectively, in the *Federal Register* and *Congressional Record*.

26. David D. Lloyd to President Truman, January 5, 1955; Truman Papers, PPS (Name File), Box 52.

27. *New York Times*, May 8, 1954, p. 54.

28. "Background Information, The Harry S. Truman Library"; Truman Library, Inc. (Publicity Folder), Box 4; Philip D. Lagerquist, "The Harry S. Truman Library—A New Research

Center for the Middle West," *Journal of the Central Mississippi Valley American Studies Assoc.*, No. 1 (Spring 1960), pp. 3,7.

29. *New York Times*, May 28, 1955, p. 33.

30. Draft [of letter to contributors], David Lloyd; Truman Library, Inc., Box 22.

31. David D. Lloyd to Raymond Harkrider, August 12, 1959; Truman Library, Inc. (Miscellaneous Folder), Box 19; Margaret Truman, *Harry S. Truman*, p. 562.

32. "New Design for Truman Library," May 5, 1955, and November 7, 1955; Truman Library, Inc. (Publicity Folder), Box 4.

33. "Articles of Incorporation," May 23, 1957; Papers of David D. Lloyd (Truman File), Truman Library, Box 16; "Truman Library Institute for National and International Affairs," June 17, 1957; Truman Library, Inc. (Publicity Folder), Box 5.

34. Minutes of the Harry S. Truman Library Institute for National and International Affairs, July 5, 1957; Truman Library, Inc., Box 27; Lagerquist, "The Truman Library Institute: The First Thirty Years."

35. U.S. Cong., House, *Hearing Before the Subcommittee on the Library of the Committee on House Administration* (H.R. to Organize and Microfilm the Papers of Presidents of the United States), 85th Cong., 1st. Sess. June 21, 1957 (1957), pp. 2-3. (Italics added.)

36. Harry S. Truman, "Me and Libraries," *College and Research Libraries* Vol. 19 (March 1958), pp. 100-03; *Hearing Before the Subcommittee on the Library of the Committee on House Administration*, pp. 3-4.

37. Sam Rayburn to President Truman, July 20, 1957; Truman Papers, PPF (Name File), 1954-61, Box 72.

38. Board Members to Dean Rusk, October 17, 1957; Truman Library, Inc. (Rockefeller Foundation Folder), Box 27. The "Bemis collection," which consisted of some 3,100 books on diplomatic history, in addition to several thousand pamphlets and reprints on foreign affairs, augmented the library's initial acquisitions in this field, as Samuel Flagg Bemis of Yale had long been recognized as an authority in this field.

39. *New York Times*, February 9, 1958, p. 76.
40. David D. Lloyd to Eliot Clark, December 31, 1957; Truman Library, Inc. (Benton Mural Folder), Box 50; F. Heller, "Truman," *The History Makers*, p. 331.
41. Agreement Signed for Mural Painting in Truman Library, June 6, 1958; Truman Papers, PPF (Trip File), Box 17.

CHAPTER 4: THE PRESIDENCY AND THE DEMOCRATIC
ADVISORY COUNCIL

1. *Truman Speaks* p. 4. (Italics added.)
2. Memorandum of Press Conference Statement, August 15, 1956, Truman Papers, PPF (Name File), Box 80; J. Giglio, "Harry S. Truman and the Multifarious Ex-Presidency," *Presidential Studies Quarterly*, p. 245; Truman, *Mr. Citizen*, p. 70.
3. Truman to Adlai E. Stevenson, November 21, 1956; Truman Papers, PPF (Name File), Box 80.
4. Mrs. Eugene Meyer to Adlai Stevenson, April 15, 1958; cited in *The Papers of Adlai E. Stevenson, Vol. VII: Continuing Education and the Unfinished Business of American Society, 1957-1961*; edited by Walter Johnson (Boston: Little, Brown and Co., 1977), p. 194. Hereinafter cited as the *Papers of Adlai Stevenson.*
5. Memorandum, Charles Tyroler to Members of the Advisory Council on Foreign Policy, May 2, 1960; Draft Policy Statement, "The Restoration of the American Presidency"; Truman Papers, PPF (Political File), Box 4; *Mr. Citizen*, p. 112.
6. Harry S. Truman, Foreword to the Foreign Policy Section of *Politics, 1956*; Murphy Papers (Speech File), Truman Library, Box 18.
7. *New York Times*, April 12, 1956, p. 16.
8. Dean Acheson to President Truman, November 30, 1959; Truman Papers, PPF (Desk File), Box 1.
9. The case against Republican presidential leadership, even when the Congress is controlled by the Republican Party, was exemplified by Eisenhower's difficulties with Congress during the first years of his presidency. See Robert J. Donovan,

Eisenhower: The Inside Story (New York: Harper and Bros., 1956), pp. 142-53; for Stevenson's views, see Adlai E. Stevenson, "Jefferson and Our National Leadership," *The Virginia Quarterly Review*, Vol. 36, No. 3 (Summer 1960), pp. 337-49. "It is the best piece I've read in many a day," Truman wrote Stevenson. "I wish you would publicly emphasize what is in this article. The country needs to be told." Truman to Adlai Stevenson, July 10, 1960; Truman Papers, PPF (Secretary's Office File), Box 31.

10. A Report of the Committee on Political Parties, "Toward a More Responsible Two-Party System," *The American Political Science Review*, Vol. XLIV, No. 3 (September, 1950); Supplement, pp. 1-99.

11. Philip B. Perlman to Thomas K. Finletter, October 11, 1955; Truman Papers, PPF (Secretary's Office File), Box 23; Sidney Hyman, "The Collective Leadership of Paul M. Butler," *Reporter*, December 24, 1959, p. 9.

12. George W. Ball, *The Past Has Another Pattern; Memoirs* (New York: W.W. Norton and Co., 1982), p. 128. Eisenhower's "hired gun" in the campaign, Senator Nixon, had accused President Truman and Govenor Stevenson of being "'traitors to the high principles of the Democratic party'" by tolerating and defending "Communists in the Government." *New York Times*, October 28, 1952, p. 14.

13. Sam Rayburn, "The Case for the Democrats," *Saturday Evening Post*, October 6, 1956, p. 103.

14. Cornelius P. Cotter and Bernard C. Hennessy, *Politics Without Power: The National Party Committees* (New York: Atherton Press, 1964), 213. See also, *Papers of Adlai Stevenson, Vol. VI*, p. 374.

15. William O. Douglas, *The Court Years, 1939-1975; The Autobiography of William O. Douglas* (New York: Random House, 1980), p. 317. See also, Paul Nitze, *From Hiroshima to Glasnost; At the Center of Decision: A Memoir* (New York: Grove-Weidenfeld, 1989), p. 161.

16. Truman to Averell Harriman, November 29, 1956; Truman Papers, PPF (Name File), Box 36; Truman to Paul M.

Butler, December 13, 1956; Truman Papers, PPF (Political File), Advisory Council corres., Box 1.

17. Transcript, Charles S. Murphy Oral History Interview, (May 1971), p. 498; Truman Library.

18. Paul M. Butler to President Truman, April 26, 1957, and attached draft "Plan of Operations," p. 2; Truman Papers, PPF (Trip File), Box 12.

19. Memorandum, Charles Tyroler II to Members of the Advisory Committee on Economic Policy, November 21, 1958; Truman Papers, PPF (Political File), Box 3.

20. See, e.g., James MacGregor Burns, *The Deadlock of Democracy, Four-Party Politics in America* (Englewood Cliffs: Prentice-Hall, Inc., 1967), pp. 253-55. The members of the Council's Executive Committee included Mrs. Benjamin B. Everett of North Carolina and Mrs. Lennard Thomas of Alabama, both Committeewomen, and Camille F. Gravel, National Committeeman from Louisiana. Cotter and Hennessy, *Politics Without Power*, p. 216.

21. Memo, Tyroler to Members of the Advisory Comm. on Economic Policy, November 21, 1958; Truman Papers, PPF (Political File), Box 3.

22. Copy, *The Democratic Task During the Next Two Years*, A Policy Statement by the Democratic Advisory Council, December 7, 1958; Truman Papers, PPF (Political File), Box 3.

23. Truman to G. Mennen Williams, December 30, 1958; Truman Papers, PPF (Secretary's Office File), Box 35.

24. Transcript, Murphy Oral History Interview (May 1971), pp. 500-504.

25. Truman to G. Mennen Williams, January 26, 1959; Truman Papers, PPF (Secretary's Office File), Box 35.

26. *Where the Buck Stops*, p. 16. See also, Emmet John Hughes, *The Church and the Liberal Society* (Notre Dame: University of Notre Dame Press, 1944; 1961), p. 258.

27. Truman to Joseph L. Rauh, Jr., May 7, 1956; Truman Papers, PPF (General File), Box 7.

28. Truman to Edmund G. Brown, January 2, 1959; Truman Papers, PPF (Secretary's Office File), Box 2.

29. Giglio, "Harry S. Truman and the Multifarious Ex-Presidency," *Presidential Studies Quarterly*, p. 246.

CHAPTER 5: ELDER STATESMAN AND PRESIDENTIAL ADVISOR

1. Draft, "Bipartisan Foreign Policy—Origin and Meaning of Bipartisan Foreign Policy," September 1951; Truman Papers (George M. Elsey Files), Box 41; see also, Arthur Krock's article, *New York Times*, December 29, 1949, p. 24.

2. See, e.g., Louis W. Koenig, "Truman's Global Leadership," *Current History*, Vol. 39, No. 230 (October 1960), pp. 228-29.

3. Dean Acheson, *Present at the Creation: My Years in the State Department* (New York: W.W. Norton, Inc., 1969), p. 691.

4. Address, "The Chance for Peace," April 16, 1953; *Dwight D. Eisenhower, Public Papers of the President of the United States, 1953* (Wash.: Government Printing Office, 1960), pp. 179-188. This was, doubtless, an important speech by President Eisenhower before the American Society of Newspaper Editors in Washington, but nothing came of it.

5. Emmet John Hughes, *The Living Presidency; The Resources and Dilemmas of the American Presidential Office* (New York: Coward, McCann & Geoghegan, 1972), pp. 15-16.

6. Donovan, *Eisenhower: The Inside Story*, p. 13.

7. Speech, presented by former President Truman at the National Press Club in Washington, May 10, 1954; Murphy Papers (Speech File), Box 17.

8. Transcript of interview with former President Truman, January 25, 1954; Truman Papers, PPF (Secretary's Office File), Box 2; Truman to Joseph L. Rauh, May 7, 1956; Truman Papers, PPF (General File), Box 7.

9. Sherman Adams, *Firsthand Report; The Story of the Eisenhower Administration* (New York: Harper & Bros., 1961), pp. 130-31. Eisenhower's "Formosa Resolution" purposely left in doubt the defense of Quemoy and Matsu, resulting in an effort by the Democratic leadership in Congress to amend the Resolution, limiting the possible use of military force to the defense of

Formosa and the Pescadores, but the effort was defeated. *Ibid.* David D. Lloyd to President Truman, April 8, 1955; Truman Papers, PPF (Trip File), Box 5.

10. Dean Acheson to President Truman, July 25, 1955; Truman Papers, PPF (Name File), Memoirs File Folder, Box 1; Truman, *Memoirs, Vol. II*, p. 334.

11. *U.N. Hearings*, April 18, 1955, pp. 1625, 1629.

12. *U.N. Hearings*, April 18, 1955, pp. 1621-24, 1960.

13. Ferrell, *Off the Record*, p. 264. Eisenhower had said the same thing about Point Four to the new chairman of the International Development Advisory Board, Eric Johnston, as Truman noted on 19 August 1952. *Ibid.*; Margaret Truman, *Harry S. Truman*, p. 401.

14. *New York Times*, June 25, 1955, p. 4.

15. Winston S. Churchill to Harry Truman, 30 June 1955; Truman Papers, PPF (Name File), Box 16. Churchill's reference to NATO in this context should not be lost; viz., in the absence of the U.S. decision to resist aggression in Korea, it seems unlikely that Europeans would have backed any rearmament effort that eventually transformed NATO into a major power bloc.

16. *New York Times*, June 25, 1955, p. 4; *Arkansas Gazette*, September 25, 1955, p. 1.

17. Wayne Morse to President Truman, May 17, 1955; Truman Papers, PPF (Name File), Morse corres., 1953-58, Box 61.

18. U.S. Congress, House of Representatives, Committee on Foreign Affairs, *Hearing Before the Subcommittee on International Organization and Movements*, 85th Cong., 1st. Sess., April 28, 1957 (1957), pp. 268, 270. (Italics added.)

19. Address by former President Harry S. Truman, June 26, 1960, *Current History*, Vol. 39, No. 229 (September 1960), pp. 172-73.

20. Truman to Lyndon B. Johnson, December 11, 1956; Truman Papers, PPF (Secretary's Office File), Box 14; S. Adams, *Firsthand Report*, pp. 161-65.

21. Truman to Charles S. Murphy, August 13, 1957; Truman Papers, PPF (Name File), Paul Butler Folder, Box 22.

22. U.S. Congress, House of Representatives, *Hearings Before the Committee on Banking and Currency*, (Legislation to Relieve Unemployment), 85th Cong., 2nd. Sess., April 14, 1958; (1958), pp. 4-9.

23. *Where the Buck Stops*, p. 68.

24. Truman to Lyndon B. Johnson, December 11, 1956; Truman Papers, PPF (Secretary's Office File), Box 14.

25. *Where the Buck Stops*, p. 69. The relevant portion of Churchill's letter to President Eisenhower of June 21, 1954, reads: "In no foreseeable circumstances, except possibly a local rescue, could British troops be used in Indo-China, and if we were asked our opinion we should advise against United States local intervention except for rescue." *The Churchill-Eisenhower Correspondence*, 1953-1955, edited by Peter G. Boyle (Chapel Hill: The University of North Carolina Press, 1990), p. 147. See also, with reference to this letter, Gilbert's *Winston S. Churchill, Vol. VIII*, pp. 993-94.

26. Wayne Morse to President Truman, May 21, 1955; Truman Papers, PPF (Name File), Box 61.

27. Dean Acheson to President Truman, May 23, 1960; Truman Papers, PPF (Name file), Box 1; *Where the Buck Stops*, p. 68. (Italicized in the text.)

28. Sherman Adams, *Firsthand Report*, p. 73.

29. Mario Lazo, *Dagger in the Heart; American Policy Failures in Cuba* (New York: Twin Circle Publishing Co., 1968), pp. 171-72. In 1961 or 1962, when he was being interviewed, President Truman said that "when Castro came to power..., Ike just sat...and acted like if he didn't notice what was going on down there, why, maybe Castro would go away.... He was probably waiting for his Chief of Staff to give him a report, and he'd initial it and put it in his out basket. Because that's the way he operated." Merle Miller, *Plain Speaking; An Oral Biography of Harry S. Truman* (New York: Berkley Publishing Co., 1973), pp. 343-44.

30. Truman to Walter P. Reuther, March 17, 1958; Truman Papers, PPF (Secretary's Office File), Box 25.

31. Truman to Philip B. Perlman, February 11, 1958; Truman Papers, PPF (Secretary's Office File), Box 23.

32. Truman to Wayne Morse, November 13, 1959; Truman Papers, PPF (Name File), Box 61.

33. Truman to Wayne Morse, November 22, 1955; Truman Papers, PPF (Name File), Box 61.

34. William Hillman to President Truman, (Personal and Confidential), March 14, 1958; Truman Papers, PPF (Secretary's Office File), Box 11; *Where the Buck Stops*, p. 16.

35. Speech, Broadcast Pioneers Dinner, in Chicago, April 5, 1960; Truman Papers, PPF (Trip File), Box 24.

36. Leon H. Keyserling to President Truman, February 8, 1961; Truman Papers, February 8, 1961; Truman Papers, PPF (Name File), Box 46; Address by former President Truman in Washington, D.C., April 21, 1958; Stuart Symington Papers, Western Historical Manuscript Collection (WHMC); University of Missouri; acc. no. 4017 (Subject File), Truman Folder, Box 151. Hereinafter cited as Symington Papers, WHMC.

37. Truman to Joseph S. Clark, January 31, 1960; Truman Papers, PPF (Desk File), Box 1.

38. Truman to Stuart Symington, July 30, 1959; Truman Papers, PPF (Name File), Box 81.

39. *New York Times* (transcript of news conference at the Truman Library), July 3, 1960, p. 18. Earlier, when Truman had been discussing the upcoming National Convention with Governor Brown in Los Angeles, he said that his "principal interest [was] to make sure that the Democratic Party is not split wide open again as it was in 1924." *Infra.* Hence his strategy, it can be inferred, had been guided by historical precedent.

40. Speech to the Executives Club in Chicago, May 13, 1960; Truman Papers, PPF (Trip File), Box 25; Truman to Edmund G. Brown, April 11, 1959; Truman Papers (Secretary's Office File), Box 2.

41. *Where the Buck Stops*, p. 6; William Fulbright to President Truman, March 16, 1960; Truman Papers, PPF (Name File), Box 31.

42. John F. Kennedy to President Truman, August 29, 1960; President's Office Files, Harry S. Truman corres., Kennedy Library, Box 33. Hereinafter cited as Truman corres., POF.
43. Letter, David H. Stowe to the author [undated].
44. Truman's Schedule, October 8-October 22; Murphy Papers (Speech File, 1960), Box 21.
45. Truman To Dean Acheson, October 9, 1960; Truman Papers, PPF (Name File), Box 1.
46. Speech, by former President Truman in Abbeyville, Louisiana, October 22, 1960; Truman Papers, PPF (Trip File), Box 27.
47. Truman to Jimmie H. Davis, October 26, 1960; Truman Papers, PPF (Trip File), Box 27.
48. *Where the Buck Stops*, p. 173; Margaret Truman, *Bess W. Truman* (New York: Macmillian Publishing Co., 1986), p. 416; Ferrell, *Off the Record*, p. 395.
49. NANA article by Truman, *New York Times*, November 14, 1960, p. 1. (Starting in 1957, these articles by the former president were periodically written for the North American Newspaper Alliance.)
50. W. Averell Harriman to President Truman, November 21, 1960; Truman Papers, PPF (Name file), Harriman corres., 1958-72, Box 37.
51. Truman to Stuart Symington, February 19, 1954; Symington Papers, WMHC. "Also bear in mind," Truman emphasized, "the Republicans haven't changed a bit and you can't appease them..."
52. David Lawrence, "Truman Given Belated Credit," *Washington Star*, October 2, 1961; see also, Cotter and Hennessy, *Politics Without Power*, p. 224.
53. Theodore C. Sorensen to the author, October 17, 1990; see, for a somewhat contrary view, Herbert S. Parmet, "John F. Kennedy," *The Harry S. Truman Encyclopedia*, p. 198.
54. Truman to President Kennedy, June 28, 1962; Truman to President Kennedy, February 19, 1962; Truman to President Kennedy, January 3, 1961; Truman to President Kennedy, January 24, 1961; Truman corres., POF, Box 33.

55. Ralph E. Lapp, *Arms Beyond Doubt; The Tyranny of Weapons Technology* (New York: Cowles Book Co., 1970), pp. 92-93; Draft, "A National Peace Agency," Policy Statement by the Advisory Committee on Science and Technology, December 2, 1959; Truman Papers, PPF (Trip File), Box 23.

56. Arthur M. Schlesinger, Jr., *A Thousand Days; John F. Kennedy in the White House* (Boston: Houghton Mifflin Co., 1965), pp. 899-900.

57. Truman to President Kennedy, August 16, 1963; Truman to President Kennedy, July 26, 1963; Truman corres., POF, Box 33. A month earlier, Truman wrote to President Kennedy in a similar vein: "I would *always* like you to know that if there is anything I can do to be of help to you in the problems with which you are faced, do not hesitate to call on me at any time." (Italics added.) Truman to President Kennedy, June 7, 1963; Truman corres., POF, Box 33.

CHAPTER 6: KEEPING THE NATION STRONG

1. Harry S. Truman, "Basic Pillars of Foreign Policy," *Vital Speeches of the Day*, Vol. XX, No. 1, (October 15, 1953), pp. 12-13.

2. See, in this regard, the interesting 19-page report, "Major Decisions and Accomplishments of the Truman Administration, 1945-1952"; Symington Papers, WHMC.

3. Speech, given in Kansas City, October 16, 1954; Truman Papers, PPF (Speech File), Box 13.

4. Dean Acheson to President Truman, July 21, 1953; Truman Papers, PPF (Name file), Box 1.

5. Remarks at the Governors' Conference, Seattle, August 4, 1953; *Eisenhower, Public Papers*, 1953 (1960), p. 541.

6. S. Adams, *Firsthand Report*, p. 120; President's News Conference, April 7, 1954; *Eisenhower, Public Papers*, 1954 (1960), p. 383.

7. Adams, *Firsthand Report*, pp. 133-34; Marvin Kalb and Elie Able, *Roots of Involvement; The U.S. in Asia, 1784-1971* (New York: W.W. Norton and Co., 1971), p. 80.

8. Dean Rusk, *As I Saw It*, as told to Richard Rusk; edited by Daniel S. Papp (New York: W.W. Norton and Co., 1990), pp. 426-27.

9. E. McCarthy, *Up 'Til Now*, A Memoir, p. 127; Rusk, *As I Saw It*, p. 427.

10. For C.L. Sulzberger's able, if belated, critique of the SEATO Treaty, see his article, "The Alliance That Never Really Was," *New York Times*, May 30, 1962, p. 18.

11. The signatories of the SEATO Defense Treaty, hailed by Dulles as an "Asiatic Monroe Doctrine," and signed in Manila on September 8, 1954, included the U.S., Britain, France, Australia, New Zealand, Pakistan, Thailand, and the Philippines. In a separate protocol, the signatories extended their protection to "Free" Vietnam, Cambodia, and Laos, which were barred from joining any military alliance by the Geneva agreements of 1954.

12. Wayne Morse to President Truman, March 21, 1955; Truman Papers, PPF (Name File), Morse corres., 1953-58, Box 61. (Because of the importance of the issue involved, it is noteworthy that former President Truman held Senator Morse in highest esteem, and unreservedly so.)

13. Dean Acheson to President Truman, September 17, 1958; Truman Papers, PPF (Desk File), General corres., 1918-1964, Box 1.

14. Dwight D. Eisenhower, *Waging Peace, 1956-1961* (New York: Doubleday and Co., 1965); Appendix O, "Memorandum Re Formosa Strait Situation," September 4, 1958, p. 692. See Also, Townsend Hoopes, *The Devil and John Foster Dulles* (Boston: Little, Brown and Co., 1973), p. 446.

15. Dean Acheson to President Truman, September 16, 1958; Truman Papers, PPF (Desk File), Box 1.

16. Acheson to Truman, September 17, 1958, Truman Papers, PPF (Desk File), Box 1; NANA article, *New York Times*, September 14, 1958, p. 19. J. Giglio had also viewed Truman's NANA article of September 14, 1958, as a turning point. "This ended any possibility that Eisenhower might call on Truman in the remaining years...," Giglio added, in commenting on Acheson's

reaction to this article. See "Harry S. Truman and the Multifarious Ex-Presidency," *Presidential Studies Quarterly*, p. 242.

17. Dean Acheson to President Truman, February 12, 1959; Truman Papers, PPF (Desk File), Box 1.

18. Truman to Dean Acheson, October 14, 1958; Truman Papers, PPF (General File), Gen. corres., 1918-64, Box 1.

19. U.S. Cong., House, *Hearings Before the Committee on Foreign Affairs to Amend Further the Mutual Security Act of 1954*; (Truman's testimony), 86th Cong., 1st. Sess., May 5, 1959 (1959), pp. 1688-90.

20. Truman to Senator John F. Kennedy, POF, Truman corres., 1957-61, Box 33. In the category of "Great Senators," Truman had listed three from Michigan: Arthur H. Vanderberg (1928-51), Lewis Cass (1845-57), and Zachariah Chandler (1857-75), and only two from Ohio, Robert A. Taft (1938-53), and Benjamin F. Wade (1851-69); *Ibid.*, pp. 1694, 1699. Later on, however, he apparently had changed his mind about two of these senators, Benjamin Wade and Zachariah Chandler. See, *Where the Buck Stops*, p. 334.

21. U.S. Cong., Senate, *Hearings Before a Subcommittee of the Committee on the Judiciary*, on S.J. Res. 11 (Proposing an Amendment to the Constitution to Repeal the 22nd Amendment), 86th Cong., 1st. Sess., Part I May 4, 1959 (1959), pp. 6-8; Truman to Ulmon Bray, December 3, 1957; Truman Papers, PPF (Secretary's Office File), Box 2. See also Truman's article, "My View of the Presidency," *Look* (November 11, 1958), pp. 25-31.

22. *Foreign Relations of the United States, 1961-1963; Vol. I, Vietnam 1961* (Wash.: Government Printing Office, 1988), p. 16, fn.2. As President Kennedy said to Walt Rostow, his deputy assistant for National Security Affairs: "You know, Eisenhower never uttered the word Vietnam." *Ibid.*

23. John Bright-Holmes (ed.), *Like It Was: The Diaries of Malcolm Muggeridge* (New York: William Morrow and Co., 1982), p. 528.

24. R. Ferrell, *Off the Record*, p. 395.

25. Dean Acheson to President Truman, October 3, 1966;

reprinted in *Among Friends: Personal Letters of Dean Acheson,* p. 281. See also, Barry M. Goldwater with J. Casserly, *Goldwater* (New York: Doubleday, 1988), pp. 134-37.

26. Truman to Dean Rusk, April 28, 1961; Dean Rusk to President Truman, April 25, 1961; Truman Papers, PPF (Secretary's Office File), Box 28.

27. Christopher Andrew and Oleg Gordievsky, *KGB: The Inside Story of Its Foreign Operations from Lenin to Gorbachev* (New York: Harper and Collins, Publishers, 1990), pp. 468-69; *Ibid.*

28. Sidney W. Souers to President Truman, December 27, 1963; Truman Papers, PPF (Secretary's Office File), Box 31. the invasion force, however, represented more than a "handful of men." Known as Brigade 2506, including an air squadron, it composed 1,443 men. See, especially, the account of that venture in M. Lazo's, *Dagger in the Heart,* pp. 259-302. and see, M. Miller, *Plain Speaking; An Oral Biography of Harry S. Truman,* p. 392.

29. Andrew and Gordievsky, *KGB: The Inside Story of Its Foreign Operations from Lenin to Gorbachev,* p. 469; H. Trivers, *Three Crises in American Foreign Affairs and a Continuing Revolution,* pp. 60-61. (Italics are Trivers'.)

30. John Kenneth Galbraith, *Ambassador's Journal; A Personal Account of the Kennedy Years* (Boston: Houghton Mifflin Co., 1969), p. 242.

31. Statement by former President Harry S. Truman, October 27, 1962; Truman Papers, PPF (Name File), Missile Crisis Folder, Box 14. (Italics are Truman's.)

32. *Where the Buck Stops,* p. 190; Robert F. Kennedy, *Thirteen Days; A Memoir of the Cuban Missile Crisis* (New York: New American Library, 1969), p. 110.

33. Trivers, *Three Crises in American Foreign Policy and a Continuing Revolution,* pp. 94, 104-09; Andrew and Gordievsky, *KGB: The Inside Story of Its Foreign Operations from Lenin to Gorbachev,* p. 491.

34. U.S. Cong., Senate, *Hearings Before the Subcommittee on National Policy Machinery of the Committee on Government*

Operations, 86th Cong., 2nd. Sess., Part IV (1960), May 10, 1960, p. 566.

35. Truman to Wayne Morse, March 14, 1963; Truman Papers, PPF (Name File), Morse corres., 1962-64, Box 61.

36. Arthur M. Schlesinger, Jr., "Kennedy, John F." (May 29, 1917-Nov. 22, 1963) *Dictionary of American Biography, Supp. Seven, 1961-65*; John A. Garraty, Editor (New York: Charles Scribner's Sons, 1981), p. 422.

37. Truman to Stuart Symington, November 26, 1963; Truman to Stuart Symington, November 4, 1963; Symington Papers, WHMC.

38. George Reedy, *Lyndon B. Johnson; A Memoir* (New York: Andrew and McMeel, Inc., 1982), p. 146; Truman to President Johnson, February 16, 1964; Truman Papers, PPF (Secretary's Office File), Box 15.

39. Truman, *Mr. Citizen*, p. 263; Truman, *Memoirs, I*, p. 12.

40. E. McCarthy, *Up 'Til Now; A Memoir*, p. 177; Reedy, *Lyndon Johnson; A Memoir*, p. 150. See also Goldwater and Casserly, *Goldwater*, pp. 232-33.

41. *New York Times*, August 26, 1964, p. 29.

42. Truman to Mrs. Warren R. Austin, November 6, 1964; Truman Papers, PPF (Name file), Box 5.

43. "Truman Asks Patience in South Vietnam," *Kansas City Star*, January 24, 1965 (Verticle File); see also the unedited copy of this article, dated January 15, 1965 (Vertical File), Book Coll., Truman Library; Reedy, *Lyndon Johnson; A Memoir*, p. 149.

44. Truman to Stuart Symington, March 28, 1967; Symington Papers, WHMC. For "the cataclysmic break-up of the Communist monolith," though "never properly" utilized "in the formulation of [Johnson's] Vietnam policy," see Trivers, *Three Crises in American Foreign Affairs and a Continuing Revolution*, pp. 105-07.

CHAPTER 7: AMBASSADOR OF GOODWILL (1956-64)

1. R. Ferrell, *Off the Record*, pp. 325-26; M. Truman, *Harry S. Truman*, p. 569.

2. Daniel Longwell to Lord Moran, April 13, 1956; Truman Papers, PPF (Trip File), Folder 2, Box 2.

3. Truman to Winston S. Churchill, March 24, 1956; Churchill to Harry S. Truman, March 8, 1956; Truman Papers, PPF (Trip File), Box 8.

4. *New York Times*, April 11, 1956, p. 14; William Hillman to President Truman, (Personal and Confidential), March 24, 1956; Truman Papers, PPF (Name File), Hillman corres., 1953-57, Box 39.

5. For Truman's diary entries, see *Off the Record*, pp. 325-338.

6. Truman to John J. McCloy, May 2, 1956; John J. McCloy to President Truman, April 25, 1956; Truman Papers, PPF (Trip File), Folder 2, Box 7.

7. *Off the Record*, p. 328; "Bon Voyage," *The New Yorker*, May 19, 1956, p. 24.

8. *New York Times*, May 19, 1956, p. 11. While he stressed the importance of establishing full diplomatic ties with the Vatican, Mr. Truman also "stressed that he was 'a good Baptist.'" *Ibid.*

9. Bernard Berenson, *Sunset and Twilight; From the Diaries of 1947-1958*; Edited by Nicky Mariano; Intro. by Iris Origo (New York: Harcourt, Brace and World, 1963), p. 436. For Truman's comments on Berenson, see *Off the Record*, p. 329, and M. Miller, *Plain Speaking; An Oral Biography of Harry S. Truman*, pp. 359-61.

10. Editorial, *IlGiornale D'Italia*, May 18, 1956; Truman Papers, PPF (Trip File), Box 6; Leon H. Keyserling, "Harry S. Truman: The Man and the President," *Harry S. Truman: The Man From Independence*; Edited by William L. Levantrosser (New York: Greenwood Press, 1986), p. 237.

11. Truman to Stuart Symington, May 28, 1956; Symington Papers, WHMC; *Off the Record*, p. 331.

12. Truman to Charles S. Murphy, June 2, 1956; Charles S. Murphy to Harry S. Truman, May 21, 1956; Truman Papers, PPF (Trip File), Folder 12, Box 4.

13. Elise K. Kirk, *Music at the White House: A History of the American Spirit* (Urbana: University of Illinois Press, 1986), pp. 256-66; *Off the Record*, p. 331; Article by Harry S. Truman, "Fifth in a Series of Articles from Europe," June 7, 1956; Truman Papers, PPF (Trip File), Box 1.

14. *Off the Record*, p. 333.

15. *New York Times*, June 13, 1956, p. 5; *Off the Record*, p. 335.

16. Article by Harry S. Truman, "Eighth in a Series of Articles from Europe," June 17, 1956; Truman Papers, PPF (Trip File), Box 8.

17. *New York Times*, June 22, 1956, p. 1.

18. Pilgrims Address, Harry S. Truman, June 21, 1956; Truman Papers, PPF (Trip File), Folder 12, Box 4; *New York Times*, June 22, 1956, p. 2; Remarks by former President Truman, at Christ Church, Oxford, June 20, 1956; Truman Papers, PPF (Trip File), Box 2.

19. Truman's notes, June 24, 1956; Truman Papers, PPF (Trip File), Folder 1, Box 8; *Off the Record*, p. 337.

20. Truman to Sir Winston Churchill, July 16, 1956; Truman Papers, PPF (Name File), Gen. corres., 1953-56, Box 16.

21. *New York Times*, June 20, 1958, p. 9; see transcript of Truman's talk to the Foreign Relations Council, July 5, 1956, p. 3; Truman Papers, PPF (Trip File), Box 4; *New York Times*, May 27, 1958; p. 8; *Off the Record*, p. 361. The "French crisis" stemmed from the fall of the Fourth French Republic in May 1958, following the Algiers *putsch* on 13 May 1958.

22. Statement by Harry S. Truman, Cannes, France, July 1, 1958; Truman Papers, PPF (Secretary's Office File), Box 9; *New York Times*, July 2, 1958, p. 18.

23. Truman to Senator Mike Monroney, July 18, 1958; Senator Mike Monroney to President Truman, May 20, 1958; Truman Papers, PPF (Secretary's Office File), Box 21. In marked contrast, e.g., to the former president's likely reception abroad, see Eisenhower's reaction to his vice president's turbulent visit to South America in May 1958, in *Waging Peace, 1956-1961* (New York: Doubleday and Co., 1965), pp. 519-20.

24. Truman to Frank Conniff, January 14, 1960; Truman Papers, PPF (Secretary's Office File), Box 3.

25. Truman to President John F. Kennedy, June 30, 1961; Kennedy to President Truman, June 19, 1961; Memorandum, L.D. Battle (State) for Ralph Dungan (White House), Subj.: "Invitation to former President and Mrs. Truman to Visit Greece," May 16, 1961; Truman corres., POF, Box 33.

26. Truman to Prime Minister C. Karamanlis, May 31, 1963; Truman Papers, PPF (Name File), Box 34; *New York Times*, March 14, 1964, p. 2.

CHAPTER 8: POST-MEMOIRS ACCOUNTS AND THE PEACE INSTITUTE

1. L. D. Keyserling, "Harry S. Truman: The Man of Independence," *Harry S. Truman: The Man of Independence*, p. 238; transcript of author's conversation with David H. Stowe, January 12, 1991.

2. *Truman Speaks*, pp. 5, 37-39.

3. John G. Palfrey to President Truman, May 17, 1959; Truman Papers, PPF (Secretary's Office File), Box 5; *Truman Speaks*, pp. 60-61.

4. Address by former President Truman, June 26, 1960, *Current History*, Vol. 39, No. 229 (September 1960), pp. 172-74.

5. Truman, *Mr. Citizen*, pp. 221-22; *Truman Speaks*, p. 5.

6. *Mr. Citizen*, p. 225. The reader is referred to Chapter 15 in its entirety.

7. *Truman Speaks*, p. 6. For his thoughts on the Pentagon and military spending, see M. Miller, *Plain Speaking: An Oral Biography of Harry S. Truman*, pp. 170, 391.

8. Miller had been stung by the criticism of his book by historians, as *Plain Speaking* had not been documented. That this was indeed the case helps explain the voluminous documentation of his subsequent books on Lyndon Johnson and Dwight Eisenhower. *Lyndon, An Oral Biography* (New York: Putnam, 1980), contains more than 35 pages of notes, and *Ike the Soldier: As They Knew Him* (New York: Putnam, 1987), possibly his best

book, is also well-documented. Also, see John Hersey, *Aspects of the Presidency* (New Haven: Ticknor & Fields, 1980), p. 9.

    9. "Finding Aid for Truman-Miller Interviews," Lyndon Baines Johnson Library, Austin. Miller's interviews with Mr. Truman number 11 tapes in all, though a few of the tapes are duplicates.

    10. Miller, *Plain Speaking*, pp. 16, 18. (Miller's italics.)

    11. Miller, *Plain Speaking*, pp. 135, 415.

    12. *Where the Buck Stops*, pp. 4, 134. The phrase "a handbook for Presidents" is used by Helen Thomas in her review of *Where the Buck Stops*; the *New York Times Book Review*, December 31, 1989, p. 15.

    13. *Where the Buck Stops*, pp. 16, 273, 300-02. 345, 347; Leon H. Keyserling to President Truman, March 25, 1961; Truman Papers, PPF (Name File), Box 46.

    14. Miller, *Plain Speaking*, p. 413n.; *Where the Buck Stops*, pp. 210, 243.

    15. *Where the Buck Stops*, pp. 192, 201-02. The regimes so identified in this context are "Russia and China." *Ibid.*

    16. *Where the Buck Stops*, pp. 202-03, 368.

    17. Truman to Trygivie Lie, May 6, 1966; Truman Papers, PPF (Center for the Advancement of Peace), Box 1; Truman to Stanley S. Langendorf, October 26, 1965; Truman Papers, PPF (Miscellaneous corres., on Peace Center), Box 2.

    18. D. Rusk, *As I Saw It*, pp. 381-82.

    19. Apparently, the originator of the project was Stanley S. Langendorf of San Francisco; see Louis H. Boyar to Charles Hipsh, September 30, 1965; Truman Papers, PPF (Miscellaneous corres. on Peace Center), Box 2.

    20. Speech by Eliahu Elath at the inaugural of the Harry S. Truman Center for the Advancement of Peace in Jerusalem, held in Independence, Missouri, January 20, 1966; Truman Papers, PPF (Secretary's Office File), Box 4.

    21. Truman to Edward V. Long, February 18, 1966; Truman Papers, PPF (General File), Box 216.

    22. *New York Times*, July 12, 1966, p. 12; Truman to Hubert

H. Humphrey, June 9, 1966; Truman Papers, PPF (Secretary's Office File), Box 13.

23. *New York Times*, July 12, 1966, p. 12; *New York Times*, July 6, 1966, p. 9.

24. *New York Times*, June 14, 1970, p. 15; Truman to Abraham Harman, August 30, 1968; Truman Papers, PPF (Peace Center, Harman corres.), Box 1; Margaret Truman, *Harry S. Truman*, p. 391.

25. C. Andrew and O. Gordievsky, *KGB: The Inside Story of Its Foreign Operations from Lenin to Gorbachev*, p. 498. As to Truman's increasing "misgivings about the direction" of the future Peace Center, see his correspondence with President Harman of the Hebrew University; Truman to Abraham Harman, August 1, 1968; Truman Papers, PPF (Peace Center, Harman corres.), Box 1.

26. Truman to Samuel Rothberg, June 1, 1967; Truman Papers, PPF (Peace Center), Box 2; Rusk, *As I Saw It*, p. 384; Andrew and Gordievsky, *KGB: The Inside Story of Its Foreign Operations from Lenin to Gorbachev,* p. 496.

27. Message by the former president read at the Dedication of the Truman Peace Center on Mount Scopus, March 27, 1968; Truman Papers, PPF (Peace Center), Box 1; "Center Named for Truman Rededicated on Mt. Scopus," *New York Times*, March 28, 1968, p. 58; Rusk, *As I Saw It*, pp. 386-87; Andrew and Gordievsky, *KGB: The Inside Story of Its Foreign Operations from Lenin to Gorbachev*, pp. 498-99.

28. David M. Noyes to Samuel Rothberg, August 31, 1967; Truman Papers; PPF (Peace Center), Box 1; David M. Noyes to Yaacov Herzog, August 27, 1969; Truman Papers, PPF (Secretary's Office File), Box 23.

29. Nathaniel L. Goldstein to President Truman, January 21, 1971; Truman Papers, PPF (Secretary's Office File), Box 22; *New York Times*, June 14, 1970, p. 15; "Mr. Truman's Leave Noticeable at Library," *The Examiner*, March 21, 1967 (Verticle File), Book Coll., Truman Library.

CHAPTER 9: THE POST-WHITE HOUSE YEAS IN PERSPECTIVE

1. Memorandum [Handwritten], Harry S. Truman, April 6, 1963; Truman Papers, PPF (Desk File), Box 2. Truman's small monthly pension had remained the same until June 1958, when the first of several increases were made for retired military personnel.

2. *Washington Star*, August 7, 1958; (Vertical File), Book Coll., Truman Library.

3. Truman to Charles S. Murphy, July 1, 1858; Murphy Papers, Box 20; J.W. Chambers, II, "Presidents Emeritus," *American Heritage* (June/July 1979), p. 22.

4. Robert Sherrod, "A day in a former President's busy life," *Saturday Evening Post*, June 13, 1964, p. 16; Truman, *Mr. Citizen*, pp. 123-24. See also, Chambers, "Presidents Emeritus," *American Heritage*, p. 24.

5. Robert L.D. Davidson to the Honorable Harry S. Truman, June 11, 1964; [author's copy provided by Westminster College]; *Westminster Report*, Vol. XLIX, No. 6, June 6, 1964; *Fulton Daily Sun-Gazette*, Vol. 77, No. 135, June 8, 1964, p. 1.

6. Arthur Holly Compton, who had been appointed to President Truman's "Interim Committee" in 1945, had frequently used this phrase in his speeches after 1945, but the apt phrase could also be applied to Truman's ideas on "general or liberal education."

7. James C. Clark, *Faded Glory: Presidents Out of Power* (New York: Praeger Publishers, 1985), p. 142; Sherrod, "A day in a former President's busy life," *Saturday Evening Post*, June 13, 1964, p. 18; Truman, *Mr. Citizen*, pp. 57-58. Twenty-five years later, in October 1989, ex-Republican President Ronald Reagan went even further, when he rented out the "prestige of the office" by making public relations endorsements for a Japanese conglomerate, Fugisankei Communications, for two million dollars. See Pat Choate, *Agents of Influence* (New York: Simon & Schuster, 1991, 1990), pp. 176-77. The Founding Fathers, as Choate concludes, "were worldly men." Yet they could not

"have foreseen that ex-Presidents might turn to blatant commercialism after leaving office"; Choate, *Agents of Influence*, p. 180.

8. *U.N. Hearings*, April 18, 1955, p. 1960. One inference seems to be that such an amendment to the U.N. Charter would guard against the "special interests" in any country or countries from trying to impose its own version or idea of world order upon the rest.

9. Speech, "The Presidency," n.d.; Truman Papers, PPF (Name File), F.H. Heller Folder, Box 38.

10. The same point is succinctly made by David McCullough in his brief essay, "The Man of Independence: Harry S. Truman in Retirement" in *Farewell to the Chief: Former Presidents in American Public Life*, edited by Richard Norton Smith and Timothy Walch (Worland: High Plains Publishing Co., 1990), p. 51. For a full-blown analysis of the problem of "special interests"—not unlike what Truman had warned about after 1953—the reader is referred to a nine-part series by Donald L. Barlett and James B. Steele, entitled "America: What went wrong?", published in *The Philadelphia Inquirer*, October 20-28, 1991.

11. Donald R. McCoy, "Be Yourself: Harry S. Truman as a Former President," *Farewell to the Chief*, p. 57.

12. Margaret Truman, *Harry S. Truman*, p. 556.

13. Samuel and Dorothy Rosenman, *Presidential Style: Some Giants and a Pygmy in the White House* (New York: Harper & Row, 1976), p. 429; (quoted in).

14. Memorial Address by Richard S. Kirkendall, "Harry S. Truman: A Great American President," January 17, 1973; Symington Papers, WHMC.

BIBLIOGRAPHICAL NOTE:

This work, in the main, is based on the unpublished sources of the Harry S. Truman Library in Independence. The extensive Post-Presidential Files (PPF) from 1953 to 1972 are divided into several categories: the Secretary's Office File, Name File, Trip File, Speech File, Political File and Desk File, being among the most important. The PPF includes the small Peace Center collection relating to the Truman Center for the Advancement of Peace in Jerusalem. There are also a few other collections on Truman's post-White House years, as the Papers of David D. Lloyd and Charles S. Murphy. The former relate to Lloyd's duties as executive director of the Harry S. Truman Library, Inc., until his death in 1962, while the latter include Murphy's activities on the Democratic Advisory Council and as a speechwriter for Truman throughout these years. Likewise relevant are the Stuart Symington Papers, though not all of the Truman-Symington correspondence can be found in the PPF, as the Symington Papers belong to the Western Historical Manuscript Collection at the University of Missouri in Columbia.

The most ambitious effort to bring together the unpublished letters, diary entries, and memorandum of Mr. Truman is to be found in *Off the Record: The Private Papers of Harry S. Truman* (New York: Harper and Row, 1980), edited by Robert H. Ferrell, though only the last part of this book concerns Truman's retirement years. In addition, though the Truman-Churchill correspondence for the period remains to be published, the Churchill-Eisenhower correspondence, 1953-55, can be usefully consulted along with Martin Gilbert's last volume in his official life of Winston S. Churchill. Thus, see *The Churchill-Eisenhower Correspondence, 1953-1955*, edited by Peter G. Boyle (Chapel Hill: The University of North Carolina Press, 1990), and Martin Gilbert, *Winston S. Churchill; Vol. VIII: 'Never Despair' 1945-1965* (Boston: Houghton Mifflin Co., 1988).

Other useful sources, as Truman's appearances before both Houses of Congress during the 1950s, include the following printed hearings: U.S. Congress, Senate, *Hearing Before a Subcommittee on the Committee on Foreign Relations, To Amend the United Nations Charter*, 84th Congress, 1st Session, April 18, 1955; House of Representatives, *Hearing Before a Special Subcommittee of the Committee on Government Operations* (To Provide for the Acceptance and Maintenance of Presidential Libraries), 84th Congress, 1st Session, June 13, 1955; House of Representatives, *Hearing Before a Subcommittee on International Organizations and Movements of the Committee on Foreign Affairs*, 85th Congress, 1st Session, Kansas City, April 29, 1957; House of Representatives, *Hearing Before a Subcommittee on the Library of the Committee on House Administration* (To Microfilm the Papers of Presidents in the Library of Congress), 85th Congress, 1st Session, June 21, 1957; House of Representatives, *Hearings Before the Committee on Foreign Affairs, To Amend the Mutual Security Act, Part VII*, 86th Congress, 1st Session, May 5, 1959.

Truman's memoirs, written between 1953 and 1955, were published, as it turned out, in two volumes: *Memoirs: Years of Decision, Vol. I*, had been published in New York by Doubleday in 1955, and *Memoirs: Years of Trial and Hope, Vol. II*, in 1956. His only post-presidential memoir, *Mr. Citizen* (New York: Bernard Geis Associates, 1960), and his 1959 Radner Lectures, *Truman Speaks* (New York: Columbia University Press, 1960), together with the two posthumously published accounts, *Plain Speaking: An Oral Biography of Harry S. Truman* (New York: Berkley Publishing Company, 1973), by Merle Miller, and *Where the Buck Stops: The Personal and Private Writings of Harry S. Truman* (New York: Warner Books, 1989), edited by Margaret Truman, aided in clarifying his views and activities after 1953. Among other memoirs on Truman and his views, Eugene McCarthy's *Up 'til Now; A Memoir* (San Diego: Harcourt Brace Jovanovich, Publishers, 1987), should be consulted along with three others: George Reedy, *Lyndon B. Johnson; A Memoir* (New York: Andrew and McMeel, Inc., 1982); Dean Rusk, *As I Saw It* (New York: W.W. Norton and Co., 1990), and Howard

Trivers, *Three Crises in American Foreign Affairs and a Continuing Revolution* (Carbondale: Southern Illinois University Press, 1972).

Among accounts which deal incidentally or briefly with Truman after the White House, the following are representative: *The Harry S. Truman Encyclopedia* (Boston: G.K. Hall and Co., 1989), edited by Richard S. Kirkendall; Roy Jenkins, *Truman* (New York: Harper and Row, Publishers, 1986); Cornelius P. Cotter and Bernard C. Hennessy, *Politics Without Power: The National Party Committees* (New York: Atherton Press, 1964); Donald R. McCoy, *The National Archives: America's Ministry of Documents 1934-1968* (Chapel Hill: The University of North Carolina Press, 1978).

Articles on Truman's post-presidential years have been relatively few in number with the only lengthy article being James Giglio's, "Harry S. Truman and the Multifarious Ex-Presidency," *Presidential Studies Quartery*, Vol. XII, No. 2 (Spring 1982), pp. 239-255. Other articles have generally commented on Truman's last years or focused on a particular aspect. Of the latter, two are exemplary: Francis H. Heller, "The Writing of the Truman Memoirs," *Presidential Studies Quarterly*, Vol. XIII, No. 1 (Winter 1983), pp. 81-84, and Philip C. Brooks, "The Harry S. Truman Library—Plans and Reality," *American Archivist*, Vol. 25 (January 1962), pp. 25-37. Of the former, which look at former presidents in public life, see the brief essays on Truman in retirement by David McCullough and Donald R. McCoy in *Farewell to the Chief: Former Presidents in American Public Lif*e (Worland: High Plains Publishing Co., 1990), edited by Richard Norton Smith and Timothy Walch.

Lastly, David McCullough's work, *Truman* (New York: Simon & Schuster, 1992)—published too late to have been consulted—deals with Truman's retirement years in the last chapter of this first full-scale biography of Truman.

INDEX: